GUSHUE

GUSHUE

THE MAKING OF A CHAMPION

BRAD GUSHUE

WITH STEPHEN BRUNT

VIKING

VIKING
an imprint of Penguin Canada, a division of
Penguin Random House Canada Limited

Canada • USA • UK • Ireland • Australia • New Zealand • India • South Africa • China

First published 2026

Viking, an imprint of Penguin Canada
A division of Penguin Random House Canada
320 Front Street West, Suite 1400
Toronto, Ontario, M5V 3B6, Canada
penguinrandomhouse.ca

The authorized representative in the EU for product safety and compliance is
Penguin Random House Ireland, Morrison Chambers, 32 Nassau Street, Dublin D02 YH68, Ireland, https://eu-contact.penguin.ie

LIBRARY AND ARCHIVES CANADA CATALOGUING IN PUBLICATION

Title: Gushue : the making of a champion / Brad Gushue with Stephen Brunt.
Names: Gushue, Brad, author. | Brunt, Stephen, author
Identifiers: Canadiana (print) 2025033481X | Canadiana (ebook) 20250334828 | ISBN 9781037804076 (hardcover) | ISBN 9781037805011 (hardcover; signed edition) | ISBN 9781037804083 (EPUB)
Subjects: LCSH: Gushue, Brad. | LCSH: Curlers (Athletes)—Canada—Biography. | LCSH: Curling—Canada. | LCSH: Newfoundland and Labrador—Biography. | LCGFT: Autobiographies.
Classification: LCC GV845.62 .G87 2026 | DDC 796.964092—dc23

Cover and interior design by Lisa Jager
Cover image © The Curling Group / Roberto Caruso
Typeset by Erin Cooper

Printed in Canada

10 9 8 7 6 5 4 3 2 1

Penguin
Random House
VIKING CANADA

For Krista, Hayley, and Marissa.

None of this would have been possible without your love, patience, and belief in me. More than any win or accomplishment, I wanted to make you proud.

I love you.

CONTENTS

1

SEPTEMBER 16, 2025

The first time I talked about retiring was way back in 2011. It's funny when I think about it now, given that all of my Brier wins came after that date.

We had a pretty good team back then, with Mark Nichols and Ryan Fry and for a couple of months Randy Ferbey. Kevin Martin's Alberta rink was number one in the world, Ontario's Glenn Howard was number two, and we were number three. We had some success against Kevin, but for some reason it felt like we could never beat Glenn.

After winning the gold medal at the Turin Olympic Games in 2006, we didn't even make it to the trials for the 2010 Vancouver Olympics, and that was a real disappointment. It would have been incredibly special to be part of an Olympics on Canadian soil. I remember watching television and seeing Wayne Gretzky at the curling venue. I had Wayne Gretzky wallpaper in my bedroom as a kid. Seeing him there, seeing the intensity of the crowd, really made me wish I was there.

At that time, Mark had moved to Manitoba and was thinking about retiring. We were also separating from Randy after just one season, and in any case he was coming to the end of his career. It looked like it would just be me and Ryan, and if we were to keep going, I would have to find at least two new players to fill out a team.

That's when I said to my wife, Krista, "I don't know if I'm going to continue."

Curling had been the centre of my world since I was thirteen. I gave up hockey for it, gave up golf. My only goal—and maybe some people thought I was a bit obsessive about it—was to become the best curler in the world.

Krista and I met when we were both studying at Memorial University in St. John's, and she knows me better than anyone else. It was 2001. We were both taking stats, and we just happened to sit next to each other at the first class of the year and we chatted a little bit.

That was one of the few classes I went to in person because we were on the road so much, I did most of my degree through distance learning (before distance education had really become a thing) and only showed up for exams. The next time I ran into Krista, I was out playing pool with Jamie Korab at a place called Dooly's, and I remember taking an interest in her. Then one night I was down at a bar and I ran into Krista's cousin—though I didn't know at the time it was her cousin—who I'd gone to school with from kindergarten to grade 12. Krista arrived a while later and we chatted some more and exchanged phone numbers.

Krista actually initiated our first date—she called me up and said "Let's go out." The problem was, it was the same night as the season finale of the first season of *Big Brother*, and my mother, my sister, and I loved that show and watched it religiously. I was in a real conundrum. Do I abandon my mom and sister for the season finale after we've been watching it together every week? (This was before PVRs.) Or do I say no to this date?

I did a wild thing. I invited Krista over to watch the show with me and my mom and my sister. And maybe just as wild, she actually agreed to come over, and the four of us watched it together. So Krista knew right from the start that I was pretty close to my mother. (To this day, our family still watches every season of *Big Brother* and our kids love it as well.)

She also learned pretty quickly about my love for curling. Krista was there through the early stages of my career. She went with me to my first Brier, in 2003, and she saw what the curling world was like—I was a decent-looking twenty-two-year-old athletic curler going into the Brier Patch, and all of a sudden there was a lot of attention on me. But Krista was super cool about it. She never got jealous. She never got worried. She played along and had a bit of fun with it.

The next Brier was in Saskatoon in 2004, and that was a crazy scene. It was also the first time that Kevin Martin asked me to play with him. Krista and I had to talk over whether we'd be willing to move to Alberta—we'd been together for three years at that point, and certainly any decision that I made in that regard was going to involve her. In the end we decided that we didn't want to leave home. We also both felt that I could win a Brier on my own, and that it would be more special to do it while representing Newfoundland.

I should say that Krista has been there through all the ups and the downs, the highs and the lows, and has always been super supportive. Over the course of my career there have been far too many times when she has quietly taken on extra work, extra responsibility, and extra burdens at home so that I could stay focused on curling. Whether I was training, competing, or travelling, she was often carrying way more than her share. The sacrifices Krista has made have not usually been seen by others, and too often they were probably not acknowledged the way they should have been by me, either. She held things together at home and gave more of herself so I could keep playing.

The truth is that anything I have accomplished in curling has her fingerprints all over it. Her belief in me, her patience, and her love have been part of every step of my career. She has been with me through the darker moments and has been the first person I want to see after a big win. I was the one out on the ice, but she has been part of every victory, every lesson, and every milestone along the way.

That first conversation about retirement was one of those times when she showed she knew me maybe better than I knew myself. "You're too young, and you're too good, and you have too much to give," she said to me. (Now there's also a chance that Krista tried to talk me out of quitting because she didn't want thirty-year-old me hanging around the house a whole lot more.) And then she suggested I go and have a talk with Toby McDonald.

Toby was my friend and my mentor—my guru, really—the coach of our 2006 Olympic gold medal team and also a very successful lawyer in St. John's. He was the type of guy who would rarely give me a direct answer. Instead, he'd answer my questions with questions of his own, and I would have to figure out the answers for myself.

Our conversation quickly turned from whether or not I was going to quit to what I'd have to do to keep playing and stay motivated.

"What would you want your ideal team to look like?" Toby asked me.

"I'd want to find three players who are just like me," I said. "I'd want three players who are hardworking, who are talented, and who are willing to do whatever it takes to be the best in the world."

Without missing a beat, Toby said, "That's a terrible idea. If there were three players like you on your team, you'd kill each other. You can't have four players with type A personalities like yours. I think you should go out and find three young guys who are early in their careers."

And then Toby said something that was hard for me to hear. He told me I had to become a much more patient leader. At that stage of my career, I admit I couldn't understand why everyone wasn't working as hard as I was, why they wouldn't or couldn't devote as much of themselves to curling as I did. Toby said that instead of putting everyone else in my shoes, I had to put myself in their shoes for a change.

I was upset when I walked away from that meeting, but looking back I know it was one of the most important lessons I ever learned.

I thought back to one of my former teammates, Mark Ward. He played with us for two years and my first two Briers. In fact, if Jay Peachey hadn't made an incredible shot to beat us in the Brier playoffs in Saskatoon in 2004, we would have won a spot in the Olympic Trials, and Mark would have been there with me and Mark Nichols and Jamie Korab. (Instead, we had to qualify the following year after Mark Ward stepped away from the team and moved to New Brunswick for a job.) Mark was the nicest teammate I ever had in my life and one of the nicest people you'll ever meet. He was also twenty years older than the rest of us and at a completely different stage of his life. We were young, single guys who cared only about curling. He had a wife and kids and a job.

Whenever I played with Mark, I got frustrated because he wasn't doing all those extra things that the rest of us were doing to get better. Today I understand everything he was trying to balance, and I cringe at the way I was thinking back then. He did absolutely everything he could to be as ready as he could, but his first priority was his family. He was in the gym, he was practising, he'd go to every event. Mark did all the things we asked him to do, but I was wanting more. Looking back, I feel so bad about my lack of empathy.

That's exactly what Toby was talking about.

It took some time, but I eventually did change the way I dealt with my teammates.

And I decided to keep going.

Fifteen years later, raising the topic of retirement was a very different conversation. Krista and I had talked about the future during the COVID pandemic, when we had no idea where the sport—or the world, for that matter—was heading. When it looked like the season was going to be cancelled in 2020–21, I decided to use the time to start studying for an MBA at Queen's University in Kingston in preparation for whatever my life would look like after curling.

Our team—myself, Mark Nichols, Brett Gallant, and Geoff Walker—wound up going back to play in the "Calgary bubble," where we lived in isolation and competed in an arena with no fans from February through May 2021. Eventually I finished my degree. In 2022, when we won the bronze medal at the Beijing Olympics, I could have quit. But we went on to win the Brier that year and then lose in the final of the world championships, and I felt I was still at the top of my game with some business still unfinished.

Then with Brett Gallant leaving the team after the 2022 season, and especially with the way that ended (more on that later), I was really motivated to try to win another Brier without him—which we did.

By the time we got to the final of the 2024 world championships in Schaffhausen, Switzerland, after winning my sixth Brier, I began to feel my career was on the clock. We were in against Niklas Edin from Sweden. Both Mark and I played really well, but Geoff Walker and E.J. Harnden struggled, which put us behind the eight ball. Looking back, I think it was probably the best-managed game of my career, my peak from a skipping standpoint. The playbook kind of got thrown out the window. I ended up calling for a lot of shots that might not have been the usual ones in a particular situation, but I believed they gave us the best chance to win. Niklas and his team outplayed us by 8 percent, but we still forced him to draw the four-foot in a new path with his last rock to win the game.

Needless to say, Niklas made the shot.

I remember coming off after having played so well all week long and the only thing I could think was, “Do I really want to go through all of this again?” We'd had an incredible year—we'd won a Brier and a Players' Championship and had lost a world's final by a matter of inches—but everything that went into getting there, all the stresses, all the training, all the travel, and all the nagging injuries, was really taking a toll on me. That summer I started thinking that the Olympic year in 2025–26 would probably be it.

Curling is no longer a year-to-year, season-to-season sport. The norm since the Olympics in 2002 has been for teams to make four-year commitments. The first time that curling was a full medal sport (it was a demonstration sport in Calgary in 1988) was in Nagano in 1998. But the Salt Lake City Games four years later, with Kevin Martin and Kelley Law representing Canada, was where it really became a big deal, and that's when teams started locking in for full Olympic cycles. If you want to play with the best players you have to do that, and I had made a commitment to my guys that I'd be there with them trying to get to the Olympics in Milan Cortina in 2026.

Near the beginning of the 2024–25 season, we had issues with E.J. Harnden and made the switch to Brendan Bottcher, which shocked a lot of people. (More on that later as well.) I admit that I was struggling with both my motivation and getting the most out of our team. There were a lot of distractions on the business side of the sport and I wasn't entirely comfortable with the direction the world of curling seemed to be heading.

The Curling Group bought the Grand Slam series from Rogers in the spring of 2024 and they had some different ideas about how they wanted to build the sport. Their plan was to create a fully professional curling league—the Rock League—which would be a big departure from the way the game had been structured in the past. The most significant change is that curlers, who have always been independent contractors responsible for their own teams, are going to be part of a franchise with a general manager who is going to be making decisions and exerting a lot of control over their careers. The Curling Group also wanted to bring back more of the social part of the game that had fallen away after curlers became more serious, especially after the sport was included in the Olympics.

The Curling Group staged a kickoff event in Nashville at the end of the 2024–25 season to showcase their vision of the sport for fans and, maybe more importantly, potential investors. Fans voted online to select a player to participate in an all-star skins game, and I won. At first I wasn't sure that I wanted to go, but I decided that it would be a good way to understand what the new guys were trying to accomplish.

I wasn't entirely comfortable with the kind of party vibe they were trying to create, but maybe that's on me. The Curling Group is looking for engaging personalities who are going to connect with younger, less traditional fans, and I admit that I'm a little bit more old school. I just want to focus on being a great curler and making shots and playing the game. My reluctance to play along could be another sign that it's time for me to consider doing something else.

But I really hope the Rock League will be good for the sport and the athletes. I'm looking forward to seeing how it evolves.

And then there was the proposed reality series.

In the spring of 2025, some television producers asked me to be part of a kind of *Drive to Survive* of curling. I didn't want to miss out on something that might be good for the sport—I'm a huge fan of *Drive to Survive*, which explores the world of Formula One racing—so I decided to at least participate in the pilot episode.

I sat down for an interview and the first question was: "Why don't people like Brad Gushue?" That was red flag number one.

I'd like to think that I'm well liked in the curling world, although I would understand, because we've had a lot of success, that there might be some resentment. I didn't like Kevin Martin for a long time because he kept beating me. He was the best in the world, and that was what I wanted to be. But once I got to know Kevin, I found out that he was a really good guy, and we have had a great relationship ever since.

I know there can be a bit of competitive tension on the ice, and I certainly understand it, but I've always been as kind as I can be to the other curlers. I don't socialize much on tour. I'm not around other players a lot outside of the rink. But those are the only reasons I could think of why other players wouldn't like me. I'm sure there are some people I've rubbed the wrong way over the years, but I hope most would say that I have been fair and respectful.

Obviously, the producers of the show were trying to create a little bit of drama, some kind of rivalry narrative. That became even clearer when they asked me how I felt about Brad Jacobs.

To be honest, I don't know Brad very well on a personal level. On the ice, when he's one of your biggest competitors, you have to have that little bit of hatred. You want to beat him and at times you hope he loses. That's normal in sports. But I don't know how he is with his family, how he is with his friends. I'm not able to make any judgment on who he is as a person. And that was my answer.

The producers came back to me a few months later and said that they had interest from CBC, CBS, the BBC, and the Olympic Channel and that they needed to confirm that I was willing to be part of the series, or it might not happen.

I was reluctant to commit because of my experience during the interview and I told them that I wanted to see the pilot they had produced to show the networks. By then I had started hearing rumours that Brad had said some pretty harsh things about me during his interview. I kept asking the producers and they kept stalling and pushing me to sign a contract. They said I needed to be part of it, but still, no pilot. I told them there was no way I was going to participate unless I saw it.

Finally they sent it to me. I didn't watch it—at least not right away—but Krista did and so did Brendan Bottcher. And they confirmed a lot of what I'd heard about it. Brad said he didn't like me and called me a "prick" and a "phony" because we had cut his cousin E.J. Harnden from our team.

When I finally listened to my own interview, I realized that every single one of my quotes was cut to fit into the narrative that the producers had wanted to create. (They may well have done the same thing with Brad's interview.) They were pushing the on-ice rivalry, and I was fine with that. But the off-ice animosity, the alleged dislike between players, was manufactured, at least from my perspective.

In the captions under our images in the pilot, they'd also given the players nicknames. Mine was "The Machine."

I'd be fine with it if they called me that because of my curling ability, the fact that for a long time I have competed at a high level. But I don't think that's what they were after. They were trying to cast me as an emotionless, robotic curling automaton.

Anybody, even if they've only watched me from a distance, knows that's not me.

During a game, I try to stay pretty level headed. But when we win or when we lose, I have always shown plenty of emotion. People have seen me cry after games several times during my career. I wear my heart on my sleeve. I've broken brooms in frustration. And during interviews, I'm open and honest and say how I feel to the point that sometimes I've pissed people off, especially at Curling Canada.

So that "Machine" label was manufactured, especially when you consider that the same people decided to label Brad Jacobs as "The Everyman." The good old boy versus the curling robot.

I'm the first to admit that I'm not the "everyman," at least in terms of my curling career. Not everybody has been willing to make the sacrifices that I've made or some of the decisions I've taken. When it comes to my training regimen, my mental preparation, and nutrition, I'm dedicated to the sport to a degree that not everyone is. To be honest, there have been times when I wished I was the guy who could go out and drink a few beers with his buddies without worrying about having to get up in the morning and be ready for a workout. But I can't get myself there.

A good behind-the-scenes docuseries showcasing curling could be a great thing for the game. But I didn't want to be part of a scripted show that was going to create stories out of nothing.

I also knew that all the filming would be a real distraction. The producers were going to want a lot of time and a lot of interviews. There would constantly be cameras around, including in situations where I wouldn't be comfortable having them there. With this likely being my last season, and an Olympic year, that could only be detrimental to my performance.

If I believed the producers were going to portray me in an honest way, maybe I could have lived with it and participated in the series. And if I came across as an asshole, so be it—I'm an asshole. But I didn't want to have my every sentence cut and twisted to suit their preconceived narrative. I think there are enough characters and enough stories in curling that you don't have to go out and invent them.

I had one last conversation with the producers over a Zoom call. They spent forty-five minutes begging me to be part of the show. They tried to guilt me into it. They said that without my participation, the series probably wouldn't happen. They told me that I owed it to the sport and I owed it to my country.

I failed to understand how I was letting down my sport and my country by not being part of their reality show, so the answer was still no. But best of luck to them.

And by the way, it wasn't because I have anything against reality TV. I've already mentioned my love of *Big Brother*. My daughters also completed an application for me to be on *The Traitors*, and Jamie Korab and I signed up to be on *The Amazing Race*—we actually got down to the interview process but didn't make the final cut, likely because I would have been too boring.

When the 2024–25 season was done, Krista and I had a brief conversation about the future.

"This is likely it," I said.

I wanted to take a little bit of time to let the wounds heal from what had been a challenging year, including the sudden change on our team from E.J. to Brendan, and make sure I wasn't doing anything rash. We decided to go away on vacation for a couple of weeks before making a final call. Maybe there was a chance that I would feel better physically and the motivation to compete would come back. But that didn't happen. When I got back onto the ice for training camp in August 2025, I felt some discomfort in the hip that I'd injured back in 2016 and that had been a lingering issue ever since. If there were an iota of doubt left in my mind about retirement, that erased it.

I was forty-five years old. Mentally, I was feeling as sharp as ever, but I knew that physically I wasn't going to be able to extract any more from my body.

I remember being at the Olympics in 2006 with Russ Howard when he was fifty years old, and I saw the physical toll that it took on him—how he had to prepare compared to what we were doing at twenty-four and twenty-five. If I kept playing until 2030, I'd be fifty at the end of that Olympic cycle, and that didn't seem too appealing.

"I think it's time," I said.

This time, Krista didn't try to talk me out of it.

I knew my decision meant I was going to have to have some conversations that I was dreading: telling my parents and my daughters, Marissa and Hayley, and then telling my teammates.

My oldest daughter, Hayley, lives and dies for curling. She watches it on TV, she streams it, she knows the results of games before I do, she knows who we're playing before I know. She's a real rink rat.

My youngest daughter, Marissa, is just getting into the sport. She's a very chill girl who doesn't show her feelings the way Hayley does.

Hayley took the news hard, as I knew she would. She wondered who she was going to cheer for now. I know she'll miss watching me, and miss that connection to the top level of the game. She had direct access to the best players in the world and knew what was going on behind the scenes.

We both got a bit emotional. Hayley kept saying, "I'm sad and I don't know why."

Marissa, true to form, was more matter of fact. "I knew this was happening," she said. "I knew it all along." Somehow she had put two and two together. But I also think that because she's younger and hasn't watched me play for as long, it was natural that she wasn't quite as emotionally invested as her sister.

Breaking the news to them was tough, but after an hour or so, we were back to joking around the way we usually do.

And then I told my parents. My mother, Maureen, got a little teary-eyed but held it together better than I anticipated she would. My father, Ray, got really quiet. I know he's going to miss being the "Walter Gretzky of curling," the centre of attention every time he walks into the Brier Patch. He said he plans to stay connected to the sport even if I'm not playing, and I know the people he hangs out with will be glad to hear that.

The last step, before going public with the news, was letting my teammates know what was happening.

Mark, Geoff, and I have played together for a long time. They understand the physical challenges that I've been through and I've shared with them my mental struggle over the last year.

The truth is, they have had the same issues with motivation that I have. We still get excited about the bigger events, like the Brier, but the other ones feel like more of an obligation than anything.

I wanted to give the guys a full season's notice so they'd have plenty of time to figure out their curling futures and also to think about the effect this will have on their family life. My decision is going to have a huge ripple effect through our team, even if it might not come as a complete shock to them that I'm retiring.

I've developed and managed our relationships with sponsors for as long as we've curled together and I've done a lot of the logistics work within the team. Curling is different than other sports—there's no "league" per se, there's no collective agreement or players' association. We all arrange our own travel and accommodations on tour and make our own deals with sponsors.

If the other guys want to continue playing as a team, they'll either have to sign on with a skip who does what I've done, or they'll have to take over managing sponsor relationships, signing and negotiating contracts with those companies, working out marketing plans, and booking team travel.

But first they are going to have to navigate their way through curling's annual "free-agent frenzy." Those conversations about who is going to be playing with whom the following season are always going on behind the scenes in our sport, but they really start to pick up near the end of an Olympic cycle. Since residency restrictions were loosened in 2019 to allow one player per rink to live out of province, there has been a lot of movement as the best skips try to recruit the best players from across Canada, and the best players look for the best situation.

"What are your plans for next year?"

"Are you committed to playing as much?"

"We should look at playing together down the road."

It isn't blatant. Players kind of dance around the topic. You don't usually come out and say anything publicly until after the Brier, when decisions have been made and teams have been officially dissolved and re-formed.

After I announce my retirement plans, our guys will have lots of options. They're great people and they're great curlers. If I'd intended to keep playing, most would assume that they would be staying with me. But when the news breaks that I'm going to be gone at the end of the season, the door will be opened for them to approach, and be approached by, other skips.

I hope that it's not a distraction for them, but it's a natural part of our sport. We're going to be very open and honest about it. The guys will be free to take care of their own business as long as, when they get on the ice, they're focused on the season in front of us and ready to go.

So that's where my head is as I get ready to meet the guys for training ahead of our first competition of the year, the AMJ Masters in London, Ontario. I'll tell them first, then the sponsors, and after that the rest of the world.

Just about everybody I've spoken to in the last six months has asked me, "What are your plans after this year?" I danced around the question because the truth was, I hadn't 100 percent made up my mind.

I don't want to do that anymore. I just want to be straight with them and say, "This is it." I think people will understand, and if they don't, nothing I can say or do will change that.

I'll weather the storm around the announcement, do the interviews, and then with luck we should be able to concentrate on the upcoming season, and especially the Olympic trials coming this fall.

I'm feeling at peace with my decision.

I know that nothing I do during this last season is going to change how people think about my curling career. Another Brier is not going to change how people think of me as a curler, and another Olympic gold is not going to change how people think of me as a curler.

If people think I'm the greatest of all time, they're probably still going to think that; if they don't, another Brier or another medal isn't going to change their mind. (Growing up and competing against Kevin Martin, I always thought he was the greatest of all time. Would I have felt any differently about him if he'd won five Briers instead of four? I don't think so.)

I'm at the point now where my reputation is what it is, and that gives me a little bit of freedom.

My bigger fear is what is going to fill the void in my life. It's going to be a huge gap.

I never felt that I was a "professional curler." I always had a job outside of the sport. I've owned and run businesses, and I've always had other ways to make money.

But curling has been my driving passion. It was all I thought about even when I was doing those other jobs that allowed me to continue to curl. What I ate, what I did throughout the day, the workouts, making sure I got enough rest—all of that was focused on allowing me to be the best curler I could be. I would sit down for Christmas dinner and not eat all the good stuff because I wanted to be ready to get back on the ice on Boxing Day—or even on

Christmas night. When I went out with my buddies on a Friday night on George Street, I was the one who went home early and went to bed so I could get a good night's sleep because I had to train in the morning. Every decision I made, the focus was "How is this going to impact my curling?"

What was the driving force that pushed me to be in the best shape I could be, to make good decisions, to be the best player in the world? The truth is, I don't know. And the other truth is that if I did know, if I had another passion that I could just plug in to replace curling, I'd feel a whole lot more comfortable than I do right now. But I don't, and so it feels a little bit like I'm jumping out of a plane with no parachute and there's nothing to catch me.

I will still stay engaged with curling on some level—playing mixed doubles with my daughters or doing some work in the media. But I also want to find something else where I have close to the passion I had for curling, something that can push me day in and day out to make the kind of tough decisions that I made in my curling career.

Another sport? Maybe. But I'm not sure there's a sport I could do just for fun. I'll give you an example. As a teenager, I was a nationally ranked golfer. I won the provincial championship in Newfoundland. I was incredibly good for my age. But then I made the decision to focus on curling and quit golf cold turkey. I didn't play at all for five or six years.

And then when I went back and played for fun, I wasn't as good because I wasn't putting in the time. I was ten shots worse than I had been as a kid. It still frustrates the hell out of me every time I go onto the golf course, not being able to pull off shots that used to be easy for me.

I may be getting better at handling that frustration, but there are still times on the golf course where I become infuriated that

I can't make a flop shot over a bunker that I could make when I was sixteen or seventeen years old.

So imagine me going out after I retire and curling with a few buddies on a Wednesday night and not being able to draw the four-foot on command or make a simple runback. I'd be so mad at myself. Logically it would make sense because I wouldn't be putting in the time and effort anymore, but I don't think a reasonable explanation would change how I was feeling. It would drive me crazy.

The fun part of sports for me has always been getting better and seeing the improvement in my performance. That's what pushes me and that's where the pleasure comes from.

The moment I love the most—and I know this may seem pretty strange to some of you—is going to the curling rink when nobody else is there. The only sound I hear is the rock sliding down the ice and hitting the pebbles, that rumble, the reason they call it "the roaring game." I'm happy doing that for hour upon hour, working on one skill or another. It brings me the most joy. It is my sanctuary. It is where I find the most peace. I can shut out everything else. If I'm stressed about something, those thoughts disappear.

It's actually hard to find that opportunity back home now. The St. John's Curling Club is so busy, the ice is almost never free (which is a great thing). But last year I was in a town called Martensville, Saskatchewan, just outside of Saskatoon, watching my daughter Hayley play. I reached out to the ice maker and he found some free time for me to go out and practise.

I walked into this nice little four-sheet club, and the building was empty. The ice maker said, "On your way out, close the door and it will lock behind you."

I had the whole place to myself.

At this stage of my career, I can't throw as many rocks as I used to, but that day in Martensville I threw twice as many as

I should have because I loved it so much. It brought me back to the way it felt when I was a teenager, when I could go to the curling club when I knew it would be deserted and throw as many shots as I wanted.

When I got back to the hotel, Krista asked me, "How did practice go?"

"It was amazing," I said.

During the 2024–25 season, I didn't have too many moments like that. I didn't enjoy curling very much. Maybe, after I retire, I can get to that place in my mind again. But I won't start to think about that until after my last competitive game is over, in spring 2026.

I'm preparing mentally and physically for one last dance. There will be a chance to qualify for the Olympics—wouldn't it be something if, exactly twenty years later, we were back in Italy playing for a gold medal? And after that, a shot at a seventh Brier back in the place where I won the first in 2017—my hometown, St. John's, Newfoundland. That's going to be a scene, but I can't worry about it today.

I know there are going to be times during the season, in a certain place or during a certain competition, when it hits me that this is the final time around, and the emotions are going to come out.

It's going to be an absolute battle, and in some ways I'm dreading it. But we'll cross those bridges when we get there.

Right now, it's time to hit the ice.

2

A PROUD NEWFOUNDLANDER

I am a Newfoundlander.

I know that some of you think I don't sound much like one because I don't have an accent like Alan Doyle or Bob Cole or Mary Walsh. As the crow flies, it's actually not that far from Petty Harbour, where Alan grew up, to Mount Pearl, which is now part of the larger St. John's urban area, where I grew up in the 1980s and '90s. But even though there are just a few miles between them, it's almost like those two places were decades apart.

I think my generation marked a shift when some of the traditional Newfoundland dialect started to disappear. A lot of that was because of television. I grew up watching TV, but I wasn't hearing people who talked with that strong Newfoundland accent. There were some Newfoundland-based shows, like *All Around the Circle* and *Up at Ours*, but for the most part I grew up watching the same stuff as other kids my age in North America: *The Cosby Show*, *Growing Pains*, and of course lots of sports. The shows that are talked about as being important in terms of Newfoundland culture and identity—*Wonderful Grand Band* and *CODCO*—were all finished by the time I was a kid, so I missed that experience. My generation was very Americanized.

We started speaking in a way that sounded like what we were hearing on TV. And on top of that, the St. John's accent—I'm a "townie"—was never as strong as the accent in the outports, the smaller settlements scattered all along the province's coasts.

My parents both came from places like that. My dad is from St. Joseph's and my mom is from O'Donnells, two tiny communities on St. Mary's Bay. They both moved to St. John's when they were young, and though mainlanders tell me that they think my parents have Newfoundland accents, I don't hear it.

My mom, whose family name is Hanlon, was one of fifteen kids, the oldest girl. Families of that size were pretty normal in those days in outport Newfoundland. There were so many kids that, with both of my grandparents working, Mom took on a parenting role with her younger siblings, especially the girls. There wasn't much of an age gap between the kids (one died in infancy), but because my older uncles moved away when they were eighteen or nineteen years old, there was hardly any time when the whole family was living in the house together.

When I was a kid, my Hanlon grandparents and my grandmother Gushue lived next door to each other in two houses that were maybe fifty metres apart, just off the main road, looking out over St. Mary's Bay. We would go up as a family three or four weekends a month to visit until I was eleven or twelve years old and my sports activities started to get in the way.

Grandmother Gushue's house was one of the oldest in the community. My sister and I always thought it was haunted. It had a narrow, rickety staircase where as soon as you took a step you heard these squeaky noises straight out of a horror movie. We didn't like going upstairs and we didn't even like anybody else going upstairs because of the sound it made.

We normally stayed with my Hanlon grandparents. They had a newer and much brighter house—with no rickety stairs. There were always a lot of people around because Mom had such a big family. Everybody would go to their house on Friday night and would leave Sunday afternoon after dinner. My older aunts and uncles would get the bedrooms and the younger ones, who actually lived there throughout the week, would end up moving out into the hall along with all of the cousins. There would be a bunch of us lying next to each other on makeshift beds in the hall or on the landing. Others would sleep downstairs on chairs or couches or wherever they could find a space.

It was a lot of fun. On Sunday afternoon, my grandmother Hanlon would cook a big dinner of turkey or roast beef or ham, and there'd be cabbage and potatoes and carrots. After dinner I'd take the vegetable trimmings to feed their horse, Cherry.

My grandfather Hanlon was a real outdoorsman. He cut his own firewood and hunted. And I loved his horse. Unfortunately, the time came that Cherry couldn't work anymore and my grandfather had to put him down. On the next visit I met his new horse, a brown one named Trigger. My grandfather explained to me that he called him that because he'd had to shoot Cherry. Understandably, I never warmed up to Trigger.

I also travelled off the island a lot when I was growing up. When I played golf and baseball as a kid, I often had to go to the mainland to compete. I didn't try to change my accent on purpose to sound like the people there, but you do tend to unconsciously pick things up when you hear people speak a different way.

But just because I don't sound like someone from around the bay and I didn't grow up on the wharf cutting cod tongues doesn't change the way I feel about my home. I am a proud Newfoundlander. I live and breathe it. I couldn't be more passionate about it.

Over the years I've had lots of opportunities to move away, opportunities that certainly would have been good for my curling career. Kevin Martin asked me a number of times to join his Alberta rink when it was the best in the world. There would have been better facilities and better training available to me there, and it would have been way cheaper. But I just couldn't see myself living on the mainland and putting on an Alberta jacket. I wanted—even needed—to be in Newfoundland, to raise my family here, and to represent the province even if that was the more challenging path to follow.

This place has shaped me—who I am, how I think. And there is nothing, anywhere, like the way Newfoundlanders celebrate and support their fellow Newfoundlanders. I know I wouldn't have played for as long as I have if I had not felt the love from back home.

That extends beyond the island because there are Newfoundlanders living everywhere in Canada. We've played in the middle of Alberta, in Manitoba, in Halifax, in southern Ontario, and we've been the crowd favourites because so many expats have come out to cheer us on. Even if they just have a distant Newfoundland connection in their family, they have adopted our team. It's hard to put in words what that feels like, but every time we're at an event and I see those Newfoundland flags in the crowd, I can tell you it's special.

I try to spend as much time as I can with those fans and to hear the stories of people driving seven or eight hours or flying across the country to watch us play. I've had people tell me that watching us has helped them get through some rough winters, cheering us on and living and dying with every one of our shots. They share the excitement when we win and the heartbreak when we lose. It makes you feel like you're playing for something bigger than yourself. And then there are the stories about young kids we inspired to take up the sport after our Olympic win in 2006. That's been a big part of what has kept me motivated.

It's certainly not just us. Newfoundlanders support our own in sports and entertainment and anywhere else they turn up on the national or international stage. I remember when Great Big Sea became the biggest band in Canada, and we were so excited that they were from Newfoundland. When Allan Hawco was on *Republic of Doyle* and that was the biggest show in Canada, we were super proud. When Rex Goudie was on *Canadian Idol* in 2005 or Kellie Loder was on *Canada's Got Talent* in 2022, Newfoundlanders did everything they could to vote them to the top. I feel tremendous pride when I see Mark Critch on *Son of a Critch* because he's one of us.

There's an intensity in how we feel about home that I think is different than anywhere else in Canada. Other, bigger places produce great athletes, musicians, and movie stars on a pretty regular basis. It doesn't happen all that often here, so that's part of where the passion of the fans comes from. Plus, Newfoundlanders by nature are a very friendly, engaging bunch. We don't find it hard to walk up and have a conversation with a stranger.

When we see a Newfoundlander on TV, we automatically feel like we know them. And those of us in the public eye get that a lot—Newfoundlanders who are complete strangers to us coming up and talking to us like we are lifelong friends. Sometimes they even tell us stories that a stranger probably shouldn't be hearing.

It's not like we can hide. When you see a curler on the street or sitting down in a restaurant, they look pretty much the same as they do when you see them competing on TV. We don't wear helmets or visors on the ice. Our hair looks the same. You hear us talking during the broadcasts. It's all pretty familiar.

Before 2006, I was known in the Newfoundland sporting community because our team won a world junior championship, but I could still go down to George Street and get drunk if I felt like it and nobody would care. St. John's is a small big city (or a big small town—take your pick), where you're usually likely to run into someone you know, but I still had my personal space.

Then everything changed over the course of those two weeks in Italy.

I remember one day, two or three weeks after the Olympics, when I went to the Avalon Mall to pick something up. (For those of you who live in places where there are many different shopping malls, it may be a little bit difficult to understand just how central the Avalon Mall is to life in St. John's. It's like Main Street—everybody goes there.) I got no more than a few steps into the mall before I was recognized.

First one person came up to me, and then someone else came up to me, and then there were five or six people gathered around. Other people saw the crowd and realized there was something going on. It got to the point where there were thirty or forty people surrounding me, and the crowd kept growing. I must have signed fifty autographs and had at least as many pictures taken. Just then a guy from mall security came up to me and said, "Sir, you have to leave because you're causing a disturbance."

I tried to explain to him that I was just trying to get to a store, but I ended up having to turn around and leave. I never did get whatever it was I was supposed to pick up.

That's when I realized that life had changed. When Krista and I would go out for dinner, I had to call the restaurant ahead of time and see if there was a table that was tucked away where we wouldn't be so visible. A quick run to the supermarket would always turn into an autograph session.

It was like that for three or four years after the Olympics, and I admit that at first I really struggled with it. I'm a true introvert and there were days when I was in a rush to get things done or in a bad mood and the last thing I wanted was to stop and talk curling with somebody I didn't know.

But then I learned an important lesson from Walter Gretzky.

After our team won the gold medal, we had an opportunity to visit Walter at his house in Brantford, Ontario. He was incredibly hospitable and told us stories about some of the guys who were playing for the Toronto Maple Leafs then who wouldn't give fans the time of day. If they got cornered, they'd scribble out their name as an illegible autograph and then get away as quickly as they could.

"You guys have a privilege being in the position you're in," Wally told us. "Take the time, be polite, have a chat. And make sure people can read your name."

That has stuck with me to this day. I have a terrible signature, but at least I think you can tell it's mine—you can pick out most of the letters.

Newfoundlanders understand better than anyone how we had to beat the odds to succeed.

There are a lot of unique challenges for a Newfoundland-based athlete (or a musician or an actor), beginning with geography. We are located on an island in the North Atlantic that at its nearest point is a seven-hour ferry ride from the easternmost part of mainland Canada. On a good day when we're not fogged in, St. John's is a three-hour flight from Toronto.

Early in my career, we played a lot in smaller places in western Canada, and it would take the better part of a day just to get to an event—the flight to Toronto, a stopover, and then another three or four hours to Saskatoon or Edmonton or Calgary, followed by getting into a car and driving another three hours to places like Bonnyville, Alberta, or Nipawin, Saskatchewan. And then we'd fly back home to Newfoundland and start the cycle over again. A three- or four-day event became a five- or six-day event for us, which is a handicap when you're competing against teams that only have to drive a couple of hours to get there.

That's what we did for years. We didn't make any excuses, even though it meant that we just had to go out and knock on more doors and get more sponsorships for our team to pay for the travel and make it work. Those were sacrifices we were willing to make—maybe because we didn't know any better and maybe because we didn't care.

But coming from Newfoundland has also had its advantages, especially in the early days of my career. The shallow pool of players in the province made it a lot easier for our team to get to the Brier. If we had been playing out of Alberta or Ontario, there would have been steeper competition to qualify. We certainly wouldn't have had all of that exposure to the highest level of the sport. We were playing on great ice against great teams on TV. A lot of players our age from other parts of Canada would never have had that opportunity.

It took a while for it to pay off.

We competed in lots of Briers but we weren't capable of winning for the first ten years. The depth of talent in Alberta or Ontario has always been a big advantage when it comes to putting together a rink. Our team always talked a lot about getting the right personalities and the right mix, but when you're only picking from eight, ten, twelve people it's tough. We had to find players with enough ability, but beyond that, they had to be curlers who were willing to put in the same time and effort that we were.

A lot of talented curlers came out of Newfoundland over the years who probably could have won a Brier. Jack MacDuff did it in 1976, but after him you had great players like Mark Noseworthy and Glenn Goss who kind of dabbled in the higher end of the sport rather than fully devoting themselves to it. They'd only play two or three events a year on the mainland.

We were the first Newfoundland team to take curling to another level. We did serious physical training. We hired a sports psychologist to work with us, and we played at least ten or twelve events a year. The cost was outrageous, but that's how we succeeded. It wasn't that we were all that more talented than the guys who came before us, because some of them were incredibly good curlers. But we had a different level of commitment.

Along the way we ran into all kinds of skepticism. Before we won in 2006, I don't think there were many people out there who believed that it was possible to come from Newfoundland and win an Olympic gold medal. Some of the biggest doubters were inside the sport—and I was always willing to take that skepticism and turn it into inspiration. (I guess that's the Michael Jordan *Last Dance* approach. I don't mind having a chip on my shoulder—or inventing a chip on my shoulder.)

For instance, I remember when I was fourteen and trying out for the provincial Canada Games team. In those days in Newfoundland there was a single tryout, and the best four players qualified because we didn't have enough teams in the province for a playdown. That year the tryout was held in St. John's, and there was a particular gentleman in charge of selecting the players. I'm not going to mention his name but he's still a part of the curling community and I see him around town every once in a while.

I was pretty new to the sport at that point. I definitely wasn't the best player there. I was still learning. But I thought I performed really well—as well as anybody there, even though most of the others were a year or two older than I was.

The fellow came up to me and asked, "What position are you looking to play?"

"I'm a skip," I said.

"Are you trying out for the skip of the team?"

"Yeah, I want to be a skip."

"I don't think you're a skip," he said.

I'm not sure why he said that. Maybe it was because of my age, or maybe it was because I didn't have as much curling experience as some of the other guys. But here was this old man—at least he seemed like an old man to me then—telling a fourteen-year-old that he couldn't or shouldn't be a skip.

I didn't make the team. (Mark Nichols did. And my sister made the women's team, which made it extra hard because I had to hear about all of the exciting things that were going to happen for her. Don't get me wrong—I was happy for her, but I was also fourteen years old and pretty pissed off that I had been passed over.)

To this day, I remember thinking, *I'm going to show that guy*. I kept that chip on my shoulder for a long time. I wanted to prove to that man that I was a skip, that I could be a skip.

I've used that same kind of motivation throughout my career. I don't internalize the slights, but I use them as fuel.

Then in 1996, when I was fifteen, I was named the all-star skip at the Canadian Juniors playing against twenty- and twenty-one-year-olds. And part of me was thinking, *Screw that guy*.

As I've gotten older, I've asked myself if that's really how the scenario played out. Or did I embellish that story to make it work for me? I know there have been times when I've done that, when someone has said something that probably wasn't meant to be an insult, but I've chosen to take it that way to fuel the fire.

That said, I know that this next story actually happened just the way I remember it.

I was nineteen when our team was invited to the mainland to participate in a Curling Canada high-performance camp. They assigned us a coach (I guess I should point out here that he was a mainlander), and the first night of the camp we were chatting, just making small talk and getting to know each other.

"Okay, guys," he said, "what's your goal for this year?"

I told him it was to win the world junior championship.

He gave me a look. "Well, you probably should set a more realistic goal."

"No, that's our goal," I said.

"Well, let's look at it more realistically," the coach said.

That was it. He clearly didn't believe that four kids from Newfoundland could ever win a world championship.

If you're supposed to be a coach and a mentor, how do you go out and tell a young athlete that they can't achieve their dream?

I guarantee you that I'm not the first Newfoundlander to have that experience. But if that guy wasn't going to believe in what we were doing, I didn't want him anywhere near our team. The next day, I went to the organizer of the camp and told him we wouldn't be working with that coach.

It was a tough conversation, and the coach wasn't too happy about it, but to Curling Canada's credit, they found us someone who was willing to buy into our goals.

Oh, and by the way, we won the world junior championship that year.

There is one last thing I should talk about when it comes to being a curler from Newfoundland. It's not a complaint, and it's definitely not an excuse for anything. But it is the reality.

There is a burden, a unique pressure that comes from wanting so badly to perform for everybody back home.

And as I've gone on in my career, I've found it tougher and tougher to deal with. Early on, when we first had some success, it was cool to feel the support from people in Newfoundland. But after you do it for a while, and especially after you've had some success, that support starts to become more of an expectation.

I remember coming off the plane after we won the Olympics in 2006, and the airport in St. John's was a sea of people. They were turning folks away at the entrance—it was crazy how many were there. Getting off the escalator that takes you down to the baggage area was like jumping into a mosh pit.

Then in 2017, after we won our first Brier, in St. John's, thousands of people hung around in the Brier Patch for hours after the final just to have the chance to celebrate with us. A year later, in 2018, we came back from winning our second Brier, in Regina, and there was a decent crowd at the airport waiting. After that, after winning another Brier and another Brier and winning the Olympic bronze in 2022, the crowds got smaller and smaller, until after the last Brier, there was nobody waiting at the airport.

As I've gotten older, maybe I've become more sensitive to that than I should be. I still want to represent the people back home. I want them to be excited when we win. But now that there's more stress on me, more pressure, more anxiety at the thought of having a poor performance, I know I'm not just letting myself down or my teammates down. There's a half a million people in Newfoundland—and probably at least another million Newfoundlanders living in other parts of Canada—who are feeling the same thing.

On balance I know it's far more positive than negative. I've received far more benefit than burden from the support of Newfoundlanders.

The issue is with me, how I've handled the pressure to perform and how I've felt about it in these later stages of my career.

We played a Grand Slam event in St. John's in December 2024, and I really wanted to put on a good show for the home crowd. I wanted them to be able to see us play well, rather than wanting to play well for ourselves. That was a first for me.

It was so different than the St. John's Brier in 2017. Then, I found a way, as bad as it may sound, to make it about me, to make it about winning my first Brier, and not about trying to win it for the home fans and for Newfoundland.

I knew what the reaction would be from everybody around Newfoundland and across Canada who supported us. But I wanted to win because I hadn't won a Brier before. I wanted that monkey off my back. It didn't have anything to do with the province. It was an internal battle that I was fighting.

At that Slam in St. John's, it wasn't about me anymore. It was about everyone else, and to be quite honest, I didn't handle it very well.

3

PICKING UP THE BROOM

Like a lot of people, my first exposure to curling was through television.

I was in grade 7 or 8 and I remember watching this strange new sport and being impressed with the skill it must take to throw the rock at a target 140 feet away. But what really drew me in was the strategy involved. I was playing competitive chess in school at that time and to me curling seemed a lot like chess on ice. You're always thinking about how your opponent will respond to a particular shot, and the better you get, the more you start thinking two or three or more shots ahead.

I got my mom interested in curling first—we would watch the Scotties and the Brier in the afternoon when I got home from school. Then my dad started watching, and after he got home from work we'd tune in to the night draws. Neither of my parents had ever curled or ever really paid attention to the sport before. Then my sister, Natasha, became a fan too (we only had one television in the house, so she had no choice but to join us on the couch) and we started watching together as a family.

After doing that for a year or two, my sister and I began asking our parents if we could try curling.

"No," they said. "It's too expensive."

I was already involved in baseball, golf, hockey, volleyball, soccer—you name it, I played it. So maybe what they were really saying was that they just couldn't handle driving me to one more sport. Maybe the expense part was just an excuse.

But then one day, when I was thirteen, my sister came home from high school and said that there had been an announcement about an after-school curling program. The cost was twenty-five dollars. That pretty much took care of the "too expensive" part. I could come up with twenty-five dollars on my own from my birthday money. "If you can get me there," I said, "I'll pay for it."

My parents gave in, reluctantly. And my sister and I immediately fell in love with the game.

My first day of curling, in October 1993, coincided with the end of my hockey career. The truth is, I wasn't loving hockey. I had good hands but I was a terrible skater. Those fast-twitch fibres are just not in my body.

My father had gone out and bought all new hockey equipment for the beginning of the season. Then I came home after that first time curling and said to my mom, "I don't want to play hockey anymore. I want to curl."

"Well," she said, "you can tell that to your father."

A few days later, on a Saturday morning, I was supposed to go to practice, and I still hadn't told my dad. He'd gone off to work early that morning to his contracting business but came back to pick me up and take me to the rink.

And Mom said to Dad, "Brad wants to tell you something."

"I'm quitting hockey," I told him. "I want to curl full-time."

My dad was and is a big hockey guy—a Leafs fan. He played the game and loved watching it on TV. A few expletives came out of his mouth as he fired my hockey bag down the basement stairs. Then he went back to work.

I remember telling myself, "Well, that went well."

I had to wait a few hours for Dad to cool down. When he came home he still wasn't thrilled. But as time went on, and the memory that he had wasted all that money on hockey equipment faded, he started to understand just how much I was enjoying curling. He's gone on to be my biggest supporter and a huge fan of the game. He loves the atmosphere at the rink and he loves being a part of it.

But I can tell you, that first day he was not happy about my decision.

When I started playing, St. John's wasn't a curling city and Newfoundland wasn't a curling province.

There was only that one Brier win back in 1976. In the mid-1990s most communities of any size in the province still had a curling club, but they were all on the brink of failing—and many of them did fail during the early years of my career. Places like Buchans, Grand Falls, Gander, Corner Brook, Stephenville, Port aux Basques, Botwood, Harbour Grace. Most of those didn't survive, and over a stretch of about ten years, the number of clubs in Newfoundland was cut in half.

In St. John's, there were two places to play, the St. John's Curling Club, where I started out, and the Bally Haly Golf and Curling Club, which was a much more expensive private club that also had a beautiful golf course. Most of the competitive curling took place at the St. John's club, but even it went through its own tough times.

I remember that during one of my first years in the sport I signed up to play in the Bon Voyage, which was the last tournament of their curling season. It was a mixed event, but it was mostly just a big party. I didn't realize it at the time but there was a serious financial drama playing out behind the scenes. When we got to the closing banquet, the president of the club, Eugene Trickett, got up and announced to the crowd, "We're going to be able to open next year."

They'd apparently been that close to going under.

The first year my sister and I were in the club's junior program, there were probably only twenty of us, total. (There are hundreds now, and I'd like to think I've had something to do with that.) Not long after I started, some guys who were seventeen or eighteen asked me if I would join them on a team. As a thirteen-year-old I thought that was pretty cool—the older guys asking me to play.

I was still involved in a bunch of other sports and I was pretty good at all of them (with the exception of hockey). I was part of the athletic crowd in school. But when I quit hockey to concentrate on curling, all of a sudden it was very easy for kids to make fun of me. I got teased a ton from grade 8 right up until grade 12. I won't say bullied—that's a bit too strong. Some of my classmates called me a sissy and said that curling was a wussy sport. Maybe the only reason that it didn't turn into full-on bullying was that I stuck up for myself. They knew I wasn't a pushover.

Eventually the only other sport I hung on to was golf. I could do that in the summer (which, in Newfoundland, is a pretty short season) and then focus on curling in the winter months.

When I was seventeen, in 1998, I won the provincial amateur golf championship, and it looked like I had a pretty good chance of getting a scholarship at a U.S. college. Had that happened, it would have provided a free education, but it would have required me to give up curling and focus completely on golf.

That summer I was invited to a golf camp run by the Royal Canadian Golf Association (now Golf Canada) at the famous Royal Montreal course. My roommate there was Brad Fritsch, who went on to play on the PGA Tour and had a really good professional career.

During the camp I played a round with Brad and felt great

about it—I shot even par, as I remember. I was keeping Brad's score, and when we came off after finishing, I tallied it up and he had shot five under. I had just played one of my best rounds of golf of the year and was super pumped with myself, and Brad had still beaten me by five shots. It made me realize just how far away I really was.

A couple of days later, Brad and I played with one of the pros from Royal Montreal. It's worth noting that they had hosted the Canadian Open there the year before.

We were on the tenth or eleventh hole and I hit a huge drive right down the middle of the fairway. As we were walking up to my ball, the pro was talking about how good my drive was, and I was feeling pretty confident.

After I hit my second shot into the green, we walked twenty yards down the fairway and the pro said to me, "This is where Vijay Singh hit his drive in the Canadian Open." *Okay*, I thought. *One of the world's best players out-drove me by twenty yards.*

Then we walked another twenty yards, and the pro said, "And this is where Tiger Woods hit his."

That's when the penny dropped. I was nowhere close to making it as a pro golfer. Just to get to Brad Fritsch's level, I had to be four or five strokes better, and at that point in his life, Brad himself was still four or five strokes from making a living in the sport.

(Brad and I reconnected years later, after he had established himself on the PGA Tour and our team had won the Olympics. It was fun to talk about what we had achieved after sharing that little dorm room at Royal Montreal.)

So I turned away from golf. Maybe I still could have won a scholarship and finished with a university degree free of charge. But by that point, if you were serious about either sport, year-round training was becoming more and more important, which meant the golf seasons and the curling seasons were starting to overlap.

I decided to shift my focus 100 percent to curling.

Sometimes I find it hard to explain exactly why the sport became the driving force in my life. I just know I wanted to be really good at *something*. When I played golf, I was very focused on that. But with curling, I loved every aspect of the game, the strategy, and being part of a team.

Golf could be very lonely, which to a certain extent suited my personality. As a skip in curling, you still get to be on your own a lot. I spend the majority of the game standing by myself, immersed in my thoughts, which I enjoy. But I also have those moments when I interact with my teammates, trying to make them as good as they can be—and allowing them to help me as well. I like that too.

I don't think I have an obsessive personality. What has driven me throughout my career is how much I love the game and the desire to be the best in the world. I also think I had incredible support around me from my parents and Krista and my kids that allowed me to do that. I've never had anybody pull me away or put restraints on the passion that I've had for curling.

I admit that sometimes it has been hard for me to identify my limit. I always felt that I could do more. You can make yourself crazy thinking that way—and there were times when I did make myself crazy. I needed someone to come up to me and say, "Enough is enough, Brad. That's enough rocks for today."

I'll give you an example.

Back in the 1997–98 season, when Mark Nichols and I were seventeen, the skins game was held in St. John's. It was a big deal, featuring the top four teams in the world, and it was televised on TSN.

They brought in Shorty Jenkins, the world-famous ice maker, to handle the event. Shorty used to bring his own rocks so he would know exactly what they were going to do, and also he would of course make great ice.

Unfortunately, this being Newfoundland, the rocks had to come over by ferry, and the ferry was delayed, as it often is in the winter. Shorty had to take the rocks that were at the St. John's Curling Club and find sixteen that were as closely matched as possible. He needed someone to throw those rocks so he could see how they behaved. Mark and I volunteered. We were already good curlers and we could throw the same way every single time, which was what Shorty needed. For us, this was a chance to play on the best ice we were ever going to play on.

We got through matching with Shorty after about two hundred rocks. But Mark and I kept going. We ended up throwing for nine or ten hours and probably threw five hundred rocks. I actually started to bleed between my thighs from the friction of the curling motion. (After that I had to change the type of underwear I wore.) It got to the point where a member of the curling club stepped in and said, "That's enough, guys." We needed someone to pull us off the ice.

Here's another example.

Our club manager in St. John's was named Reg Caughie. Curling fans might remember him as "Brier Bear"—for almost forty years he would dress up in a bear costume and show up as the Brier mascot. Reg was a huge supporter of our team. There were times when the club was so busy that it was tough for us to get ice time. So we'd head down at eleven o'clock at night, after all the leagues had finished, and throw. There were usually a few people still drinking in the lounge at that time, and when the last person left, we were supposed to leave, too, so that Reg could close up.

But there were many nights when 12:30 a.m. would come, and one o'clock would come, and we'd still be on the ice. Reg would turn all the lights off on us, which was supposed to be the signal for us to stop. But there was just enough emergency lighting for us to keep going, and that's when Reg would get a bit mad at us and throw us out.

For me, it has always been a few more rocks, a few more practices, a few more reps. That has always been my mentality—and sometimes back then there were times when I needed an intervention, needed someone to tell me to stop. My social life suffered, but all of that preparation made me feel like I was as ready as I could be for every game we played.

When I first suffered my hip injury, I struggled with the amount of time it took to recover. I wanted to be out working and practising and preparing. The sports psychologist I was working with tried to convince me that a couple of weeks off wasn't going to hurt me. I wasn't going to forget how to curl.

But I felt like every other curler was out there practising, working harder to get better, gaining an edge on me, and here I was just sitting on a couch. I could have looked at it from a different perspective, knowing that I needed to get better by resting and recovering. But man, I had a hard time grasping that.

The way I see it, if you want to be the best at something—or even if you want to be incredibly good at something—things have to go out of balance. And in my life, things were out of balance, and people around me had to sacrifice a lot for me to achieve what I achieved. If I needed to get my training in, nothing got in the way.

If you don't aspire to be the best in the world, go ahead and find that balance. But are you going to reap the rewards of being incredibly good at what you're doing and all the things that come with that? Probably not, because you haven't put in the time. If you don't do the work, someone else is going to do it, and they're going to be better than you. That has always been my perspective.

That's why I practised on Christmas Eve or Christmas Day or New Year's Eve or New Year's Day. I knew nobody else was doing it. I felt that I was getting an edge on somebody.

Yeah, it was out of balance. It was out of balance for a long time.

♣

In 1995, I won my first Newfoundland junior championship as part of Ryan Davis's team. A year later, after Ryan left to join another team, I became the new skip and won with my own rink. I also won all-star skip at the nationals as a fifteen-year-old competing against a bunch of twenty- and twenty-one-year-olds.

I was good, and boy, was I cocky.

The next season, 1997, was the first time of three that we cut Jamie Korab from our team. Jamie is one of my oldest friends, and over the years we have butted heads on several occasions, as I'll discuss later. But in this case the change had nothing to do with him. There was a guy on our team who we wanted to get rid of, and we approached another player to replace him. The replacement said, "I'm only coming on the team if I bring this guy with me."

So we had to get rid of Jamie to fit those two players in. It definitely wasn't fair.

That year, the Newfoundland provincials were being held in Harbour Grace, which just happens to be Jamie's hometown. As a sixteen-year-old walking into the Harbour Grace Curling Club, I was public enemy number one because we had cut the local guy. People were calling me an asshole. People were cheering for us to lose. People were saying the nastiest things you can imagine to a kid.

I felt so uncomfortable, so intimidated. I just wanted to get out of there.

Our rink didn't even make the finals, which to that point was one of the worst experiences of my curling life.

Jamie's new rink won the championship.

A year later, I was ready to take another shot at the provincial junior championship. But four weeks before they were going to start, I was in a high school gym class playing some sort of a game and I was being my typical self, going all out and trying really hard. I chased after a ball and found myself in a position where my head got over my feet a little bit too much and I couldn't keep my balance. I fell flat on my chest and hit my knee. Once I got over the shock, my first thought was whether I had really hurt myself, and whether I would be ready for the provincials.

Then one of my classmates said: "Oh my God, look at your hand!" When I saw it, I got a little nauseated.

The ring finger on my right hand was pointed out at a ninety-degree angle from the rest of them. I had broken *and* dislocated it in bracing myself against the fall.

My gym teacher, Mr. Sutton, had always been really good to me. Not realizing that the finger was broken as well as dislocated, he tried to pop it back into place. As you can imagine, the pain was really intense. He drove me to the doctor's office down the road from the school. I remember sitting there, waiting for my parents to arrive, and the only thing I could think about was the provincials.

My parents picked me up and took me to the hospital, where I had surgery. They inserted two rods to secure and straighten the broken bone. When I came to, I had a cast covering my whole hand and lower arm. The doctors told me it would be eight weeks before my finger was healed. But there was no way I was missing the provincials.

I'm ambidextrous, so I decided that I could just switch hands and curl left-handed. I realized pretty quickly that wasn't going to work. So two or three days before the competition, I went to the doctor and asked him to take the cast off. "Leave the pins in," I told him, "and I will find a way to curl." To this day, I'm amazed that he agreed to that. He took the cast off, and with the pins still in I curled with my index finger, my middle finger, and my thumb. And we won.

I got the pins out just before the nationals.

We had a good team, but our guys didn't play very well. We only went 4–8, but I ended up being named the all-star skip and winning the sportsmanship award.

A few days after I got back to St. John's, I got a call out of the blue from John Morris, who had won that championship with his Ontario rink. We had chatted a bit during the tournament but I didn't know him very well, other than knowing that he and his team were really good. He asked me if I wanted to be their fifth man when they went to the world junior championships, which were being held in Thunder Bay that year. (Teams don't take a fifth man to the Canadian juniors, but when you go to the worlds, they require you to take a fifth.)

A fifth man is there to fill in in case anybody gets injured. He has to be ready to fill in at any position if needed, so he has to be a player who is well rounded. Beyond that, their job is to help out and support the team in any way possible. Sometimes that can be as simple as getting the brooms ready. It can mean getting a drink or a snack for the team, or scouting another team and seeing what they're doing.

If there's any burden that has to be taken on, the fifth man takes it on so the rest of the team doesn't have to deal with it.

When I got the call from John, I was completely shocked. I got off the phone and told my mom, who started asking me all these questions that I couldn't answer about where and when and how. I didn't remember anything that John had said after he asked me to join the team.

I actually had to go and find someone who had his number (back then, it wasn't as simple as seeing a number pop up on your smart phone). It was a good half-hour before I managed to call John back, completely embarrassed, and ask him all of the questions that he had already answered in our first call. Mom was there on the extension as we went through all the details so that I didn't miss anything.

It turned out to be an incredible opportunity for me.

I was seventeen, in grade 12, and heading off to a world championship. The Ontario team had some really good players—Brent Laing, Craig Savill, who had a very good career, and John Morris obviously. Earle Morris was their coach. I got to play in a couple of games against Sweden and Scotland. I knew I had the skill. But, for all my self-confidence, the fact that John thought highly enough of me to invite me to join his team was real affirmation from an opponent and a peer.

We finished undefeated and won the gold medal.

And that was when the kids at school stopped teasing me about being a curler. All of a sudden, they wanted to be my buddy again.

In 1999, our rink won the provincials, then finished third in the junior nationals in Kelowna. I was named the all-star skip again, and all of the old cockiness was back.

And then came 2000, and things got pretty humbling pretty quickly.

After winning in Newfoundland, we were off to the junior nationals in Moncton. We went in feeling like we were one of the favourites. We had Mike Adam playing lead, Jamie Korab back with us playing second, and Mark Nichols was our third. A couple of the teams that had finished ahead of us had aged out, which should have left us as the best team there.

We got off to a bit of a rough start. After winning our first two games to open the championships, we lost our next two games pretty handily, which was a real shock.

Heading into play on Monday with our record at 2–2, we were feeling discouraged. That's when we first noticed a guy in the crowd who was cheering for us really loudly.

"You've got this, Brad!" he'd shout. "You've got this!"

After we won our game that morning, he started yelling, "One more win, Brad! One more win!"

I remember thinking that we actually needed to win seven or eight more games, not just one.

We went back out that night for our next game, and the same guy was there again: "One more win, Brad! One more win!"

Who is this crazy old guy screaming at us?

Tuesday morning and night he was back. Finally, I asked someone about our cheerleader, and they told me that it was Jack MacDuff.

Yes, *that* Jack MacDuff, the skip on the 1976 Newfoundland rink with Toby and Doug Hudson and Ken Templeton that was the first and only one from our province to win the Brier. He was a legend in the province, a guy I'd been hearing about since I started curling. I dreamed about becoming the next Jack MacDuff.

Jack had moved away and settled in Moncton. When we were finally introduced, he told me that he had heard through Toby and Doug and Ken that our team was really good, and that I was a skilled player, so he came out to support us.

The "one more win" thing went all the way back to the '76 Brier in Regina, when the Newfoundland team's driver was Sam Richardson, part of the famous Saskatchewan rink that won four Briers in the 1960s.

Sam was one of the biggest characters you'll ever meet. He took Jack and the other guys under his wing that week and gave them a lot of confidence. Sam kept telling them "One more win. Let's go win one more game" to help keep them focused. That's where it came from.

We got on a pretty good run in Moncton after that terrible Sunday, winning eight in a row to finish second behind Brad Kuhn from B.C. heading into the playoffs. We then beat Saskatchewan in the semifinal to put us into the final against Brad.

It was my first time in a national final and my first time on TV with the bright lights on me, a completely new environment from what I'd experienced before. I didn't handle the pressure very well, and neither did the rest of our team. That said, I don't think Brad and his team handled it very well either, because it was a very poorly curled game.

But we got to an extra end and we had the hammer coming home. All I had to do with my last rock was draw to the eight-foot to win the championship. It was a very basic shot.

I remember wanting to throw the rock quickly because of the strange way my body was feeling—the stress, the nerves, everything was building. As I was sliding down the ice to the hack, I could feel the anxiety getting worse and worse. I was thinking, *Let's get in the hack before this gets too bad, and let's get this rock thrown.*

I had really good draw weight that day, so I wasn't concerned about making or missing the shot. But I can still remember that feeling, starting from the legs and moving up. I was thinking, *If this gets to my head, I'm done.*

I got in the hack and I threw and the rock felt pretty good coming out of my hand. Everything seemed normal.

Jamie and Mike started sweeping right away, which told me that they thought the shot was light, and that made a little bit of doubt creep in. Fifteen or twenty feet down, I noticed that the rock wasn't spinning quite the way it normally does. My rotation wasn't as crisp.

That meant one of two things. Either the rock had a weak rotation out of my hand or it had picked—meaning run over some debris on the ice.

The rock was halfway to the house and it started to curl more than it should have. That took it into a different path, which meant that the speed was different than we had anticipated.

Mark jumped in to help the other guys sweep. We all knew the shot was light. And that's when the panic set in.

Halfway between the house and the hog line, the rock stopped dead.

I was completely devastated. I remember putting my hands up in the air and thinking, *Oh my God, I can't believe I just missed the easiest shot in the world to win a Canadian Junior Championship.*

In the dressing room after the game I couldn't control the emotions. I took my mic off and fired it against a locker. (In 2025, I went back to the Beausejour Curling Club, where that championship was played, and I found the dent where the mic hit the locker—it's still there. I took my girls in to see it.) My family came in, and I couldn't stop crying. I was so upset for myself, for my teammates. I felt I had let everybody down.

I eventually mustered enough strength to go out for the closing ceremonies, but on the podium I was still crying uncontrollably.

Russ Howard, one of Canada's greatest curlers, who by then had already won a couple of Briers and world championships, was living in Moncton at the time. And I remember that he came up to me after the ceremonies and said, "I'm pretty sure that shot picked."

I don't know if he believed it or if he just said it to make me feel better, but it certainly helped.

To this day, I want to believe that rock picked. It reacted like it had picked. But to be honest, I am still not completely sure. My body was in such a strange state because of the nerves and the stress that I couldn't definitively tell you if it did or it didn't. It could have been that I just threw it poorly.

That moment was a huge turning point in my career. I went home and I wouldn't leave my room for days. I was so upset and so embarrassed. I felt so bad for my teammates because they had played well enough for us to win and I had missed such a simple shot.

Ultimately it was an old teammate who helped me get out of my funk. Neal Blackmore was the second on our 1999 team, and then he had aged out of the junior ranks. He called me at home and persuaded me to go out with him to play a bit of pool. That was my first time leaving the house.

We went out, we shot a few games, and we didn't talk about curling at all. It was a big step in facing the world and getting over what had happened.

When I did get to the point that I was ready to think about curling again, I had a couple of realizations. If I got into a situation like that again where I failed in a big moment, I knew that it couldn't be worse than what I had already been through. It was a battle, but it didn't kill me and I got over it, and so I knew that was possible.

And I also came to the conclusion that if I ever had to play a shot like that again, I needed to be better prepared for the mental challenge, which was my biggest weakness. I decided I needed the help of a sports psychologist, and that's when I got in touch with Dr. Bas Kavanagh at Memorial University. I told him what had happened and I told him I didn't want it to happen again. He agreed to work with our team starting with the 2001 season.

That was a pretty revolutionary idea in curling at the time. Even after we had some success with Bas, winning the world juniors in 2001, the sports establishment didn't really understand the value of that kind of mental coaching.

One of the first things Bas asked me was, "What are your goals in curling?" I shared them with him, and he said, "I encourage you to put those on a sheet of paper and put it up in your bedroom and make yourself aware of that list. And when anybody comes into that room, make them aware of it too."

I went to Staples and picked up a big sheet of bristol board and I wrote out the ten goals that I wanted to achieve in the sport of curling:

1. Win the Olympic gold medal
2. Win a medal at the Olympics
3. Win the Olympic trials
4. Get to the Olympic trials
5. Win a Brier
6. Get to a Brier
7. Become a better competitive curler (3 percent shooting increase)
8. Win the 2001 world juniors

9. Win the 2001 Canadian juniors
10. Win the 2001 provincials

I posted that list on the back of my bedroom door so it was always visible. As I went along in my career, I was able to check those things off one by one. That's what's driven me. I was very goal-oriented from the beginning.

Bas also got all of us on the team to come up with ten positive affirmations. We wrote them out on pieces of paper and then stuck them all around our houses. There was one on the light switch going into my room, another on the TV, another on the door to the garage, and other places where we couldn't miss them. I knew that the weakest part of our game was the mental side, so I wrote out the affirmations and put them up just like he instructed. Before every game we played, I would repeat them to myself.

When you do a mental exercise like that you tend to be really good about it for a few weeks and then you kind of forget about it. But when it's on the mirror in the bathroom, it's pretty hard to ignore.

During the early days of dating Krista, she came over to the house and the first thing she saw was one of the affirmations stuck to the hall mirror: "I have incredible draw weight." And then she went into the bathroom and there was another one: "I throw my in-turn straight and positive." I had to explain to her what they were all about.

The final piece Bas added to our mental preparation was the script. Each of us was supposed to imagine how the day of the final of the 2001 Canadian juniors would play out, from the moment we woke up through the celebration after we won. He wanted us to think about everything, from how it felt putting our socks on in the morning to putting our jacket on at the rink and how it felt going over our arms, to the feel that we got under our foot when we took our first slide on the ice. The exercise was about trying to engage all five senses and then to describe exactly how we wanted the final to play out.

I really wanted it to be a close game, and I wanted to be prepared to draw the four-foot to win the championship, the same kind of shot I had missed in Moncton. I laid it out very specifically because I wanted to be mentally prepared the next time I dealt with a similar situation. In my script, we'd get a lead by one, they'd get a point, and then it would go back and forth until I had to make that draw to win.

When I got together with the other guys on the team—Mark Nichols, Mike Adam, and Brent Hamilton—it was interesting that the three of them had independently written theirs exactly the same with the same final score. In their versions we were dominant and controlled the game. We got two, they got one, we got two more, they got one, and in all three of their scripts, we ended up winning 8–3.

A couple of months before the 2001 Canadian juniors in St. Catharines, Ontario, Bas took us into a sound studio at Memorial University and we recorded our scripts so we could listen to them through our headphones wherever we went.

I guess you could say it turned out to be a really neat story about the power of the mind. We made it to the final in St. Catharines, where we were playing Mike McEwen and his Manitoba team. And the game played out almost exactly the way my three teammates had imagined it: we were dominant, we won 8–3, and I didn't have to do anything special with my last shot.

I remember the first time we brought Bas to the Brier. They have a big opening banquet where they introduce each team on stage. Curling Canada had given us approval to bring Bas as our "coach," but until then we hadn't identified him as our sports psychologist. I'll never forget the moment when he was introduced onstage.

"Here's Team Newfoundland sports psychologist, Bas Kavanagh." The laughter around the room was audible. People were mocking us.

A couple of years later, after we won the Olympic trials and won the gold medal, we were back at the Brier in 2007. And what did we see? Just about every team had their own sports psychologist on board.

That was part of a larger transformation of the sport. It went hand in hand with the new emphasis on physical fitness that came just a little bit later.

Early on in my career, I remember going into Grand Slams and it wasn't uncommon to look around a dressing room and see another player with a flask in his broom bag. Drinking during competition was common. It was an extension of the social aspects of the sport.

The best curlers in the world were still very much regular guys. If you were the best in your club you went to the provincials, and if you won that you went to the Brier. Nobody really put in the time and effort to push their bodies and push their abilities on the ice to the limit.

During the season, guys would finish their day job, head to the airport, show up at an event, play a couple games, and then go out that night and have a few beers. The next morning they'd wake up hungover, or at least dead tired, play three games, and do it all over again. Then on Sunday night, they'd fly home absolutely exhausted, then repeat that routine eight or ten times over the course of a season. It wasn't hard to find players who were more focused on the party than what was happening on the ice. They were the centre of attention, treated like rock stars. Everybody wanted to meet them.

No surprise that there were a whole lot of beer bellies.

The famous Ferbey Four—Randy Ferbey, David Nedohin, Scott Pfeifer, and Marcel Rocque—one of the best teams to ever play the game, were probably the last to do that and really excel on the ice. They were so good and they were also the life of the party on every

Friday and Saturday night at every event. They probably had more fun than any team that ever played the game. And they could still go out and curl at an extremely high level. How they did it, I have no idea.

When I was first going out on the road as a nineteen- and twenty-year-old, I indulged in the social side more than I do now, but it was never something I really loved. I don't care to be the centre of attention. And I realized that being out until two or three in the morning and then getting up for a nine o'clock game wasn't putting me in the best position to be successful. After a season or two, I decided that was enough for me. Our team started to make sure we went to bed early, ate the right things, and were prepared to play our best.

We got a reputation for being the prudes, the boring team, the team that took itself too seriously—I heard all of that early in my career. After we started having some success, those taunts turned into "You're only having success because you're not out partying with us."

Of course. That was the idea.

You can make the case that the change in conditioning really began with what Tiger Woods started doing in golf in the late 1990s. That was another game that people used to think of as more of a recreation than a true sport. Other players saw what Tiger could do on the course and saw how he transformed his body in the gym and began to follow his lead.

Kevin Martin was one of first skips to really start pushing serious fitness. Not coincidentally, he had the best team in the world. I think the fact that curling became an Olympic sport also had a lot to do with the change in the way teams approached their training. But even leading up to the 2006 Games there were still some teams on that party circuit. Ferbey was still around, and John Morris's team was pretty notorious for going out and enjoying their weekends.

By the time the "Own the Podium" funding model kicked in before the 2010 Olympics in Vancouver, pretty much everyone had flipped the switch. Soon enough it was rare to see a top curler who didn't have visible abs. And even if they didn't look the part, they were probably still able to lift and run and do all the things that you can do as an athlete. Today every team works with nutritionists, dietitians, sports psychologists, massage therapists, physiotherapists, chiropractors. Everyone is trying to find an edge, just like any other Olympic athlete.

There has actually been a push in the past couple of years from people saying we need to bring the fun back into the sport.

I'm all for fun. Everybody loves the Brier Patch, the huge party that goes on during the Brier every year. If we can create that kind of atmosphere at more events, I think it would be wonderful.

But I'm also so proud of the evolution of our athletes and our on-ice product. The players are fitter and stronger and they can make more shots and make them more consistently. It's a dramatically different game now than it was when I started out, and I think that's a great thing.

I never imagined that I could make a full-time living as a curler. It is still true today that unlike other professional athletes, most world-class curlers have other jobs.

Everyone knew that Ed Werenich of Ontario was a firefighter and that Glenn Howard managed a Beer Store. During the broadcasts, that's how they used to introduce curlers—how old they were, how many years they had curled, and what they did for a living. (I think that was part of the attraction for people who watched curling. The athletes were relatable. These were real, everyday people, not huge sports stars making millions of dollars.)

Curlers in my generation have tended to find jobs that allowed them to curl pretty much full-time during the season. We need a lot of flexibility. You couldn't be a teacher, because you couldn't get away in the winter, but we have mortgage brokers, golf professionals, jobs where you can work during the summer and get winters off. Some of us own and operate our own businesses.

When I started out, the top teams in the sport were making $70,000, $80,000, or maybe $100,000 if they had a great year. That was all prize money. You had to perform to get paid. There were no appearance fees and no guaranteed minimum. You divided that prize money four ways after you paid your coach and maybe a fifth player. All of your tour expenses—the flights, the hotels, the meals—came off the top.

It didn't take long to realize that a hundred grand in prize money shrunk to beer money pretty fast. It just wasn't a sustainable livelihood.

If we had a good year, I might have had a bit of extra cash to play around with. But it just wasn't possible to make curling my primary source of income. Even now, there are very few teams that have the ability to make serious money, and that comes down to sponsorships and endorsements, which we have to solicit ourselves.

(It makes no sense to me that we generate the TV numbers we do, we get the exposure that we do, and yet there's still so little money in the sport. The Brier final typically gets an audience of between one and one and a half million. There aren't that many other sports that get those numbers. Curling makes such good TV. There's no other televised sport where the players wear microphones and you can hear what they're talking about, hear their strategy, while they compete. Television viewers are actually much more engaged than the fans in the stands—which is the exact opposite of hockey, baseball, and football.)

From as far back as I can remember, my goal was to become the best curler in the world and win an Olympic medal. I knew that

I needed a way to support that dream, which meant that I needed a job that was going to allow me to curl.

In 1998 I enrolled at Memorial University in St. John's to earn an undergraduate business degree and continued curling competitively while I was taking classes there. I owe a lot to my professors and the dean who helped me with the challenges of distance learning.

After I graduated, I had to make some decisions. I couldn't move into a nine-to-five job with two weeks' vacation because that wouldn't allow me the time to play on tour. Instead, I needed to find a career that would give me the freedom to set my own schedule. That's why I decided to become a financial advisor. Freedom 55 Financial brought me on and I did that for a little over a year, knocking on doors, making cold calls, trying to find clients.

Try to imagine a twenty-two-year-old with no experience asking people to trust him with their life savings. I'm pretty certain that if I'd stuck with it for longer, I could have made a living. But I'm not a salesperson by nature—I'm not the most outgoing person, to start with—so it was a really awkward fit.

Once we got our spot in the Olympic trials for the Turin Games, I spoke to my parents and told them I wanted to step away from Freedom 55 and focus 100 percent on curling. I was living at home and had banked enough money that I wouldn't be a financial burden on them. They supported my choice.

But when I told the manager at Freedom 55 that I was leaving, he told me I should be more realistic with my expectations—not so focused on curling and more concerned with getting a "real job."

4

THE ROAD TO THE OLYMPICS

In the summer of 2005, my parents sat my sister and me down and told us that Mom had colorectal cancer. It caught me completely off guard. Mom is a private person, and she hadn't told us that she had been feeling unwell. The doctors had found cancer in seventeen of the twenty-seven lymph nodes that they had tested. It was a pretty bad situation. She was going to have to go through some intensive chemo and radiation.

My immediate reaction was to tell them that I wasn't going to play the coming season.

My sister was living away in Cape Breton and my father was busy running his contracting business. I had just made the commitment to concentrate on curling full-time, so I didn't really have a job. I thought that if I didn't play, I would be available to take Mom to her appointments, take care of the house, and help her get through her journey. She had done so much for me that it was instinctual for me to want to do as much as I could for her. I didn't even think about curling.

Mom wasn't too keen on the idea, but I was adamant. That's when my parents got my friend and mentor and coach Toby McDonald involved.

"Brad, you're going to regret this down the road," he told me. "Your mother doesn't want you to do this. Take her advice. Take my advice."

Ultimately, I listened to them both. We found a solution where my aunts, my sister, Krista (who was my fiancée by then), and some other relatives took on a bigger role in caregiving. That allowed me to continue playing, with the goal of qualifying for the Olympics in 2006. But Mom was always in the back of my mind. I'd call her before and after every game to make sure she was all right.

Being added to the Olympics had given curling a different level of legitimacy. When I started playing at thirteen, curling felt like a game played almost exclusively by older people. They'd have a cigarette out on the ice, they'd have a drink. It was more social than athletic. I think the Olympics is what turned it into an actual sport, though the transformation wasn't instant. But if you look at the athletes when curling debuted as an Olympic demonstration sport in Calgary in 1988 versus now, it's dramatically different.

Today, there is a push for high performance, for excellence. Second- and third-tier teams can't compete at the big events. I think that in terms of our fitness and the way we go about training, the best curlers now are on par with athletes in other sports.

The other big impact of the Olympics has been the sport's international growth, both in participation and in the television audience. With medals on the line, places like Japan and Korea and some of the European countries are putting money behind their curling athletes—more so than in Canada.

And curling is always one of the most viewed sports during the Winter Games. Even people who have never seen the game before get caught up in it during those two weeks.

The challenge has been sustaining that momentum between Olympic years. In places where you don't have enough curling rinks and you don't have regular broadcasts during the season, people's interest is naturally going to wane.

My generation of curlers is the first that grew up aspiring to be Olympians. Before that, the Brier and the Scotties and the world championships were the biggest prizes in the sport. When they made the announcement that curling was going to be a full medal sport in 1998, I was eighteen and at the rink every single day. Winning an Olympic medal instantly became my dream. It surpassed everything else.

Today, every curler's number one goal is the Olympics, and if you want the best chance to get there, you and your teammates have to make a four-year commitment.

The first year or two that a team is together involves a steep learning curve. You make mistakes, you don't know how to deal with each other in pressure moments, you say the wrong thing on the ice at the wrong time. But once you get through that and learn how to play together, you can start to have real success. Some teams even commit to stay together for two cycles—eight years. There's no science behind it, and the truth is, once you get to year seven and eight as a group, things can start to get a little stale. But time together definitely matters when there's an Olympic berth at stake.

That said, we didn't go that route in 2006. We only put our rink together at the beginning of that season, and I guess we were lucky to capture lightning in a bottle.

Once again, Toby was part of the story.

I think a lot of people know about our relationship and feel like Toby must have coached me forever. But he actually only joined us a year before the 2006 Olympics, was there through the Games, and came back to help us for another year later on in my career.

Toby was super intelligent, a lawyer by trade, with a great vocabulary and a formal, old-fashioned way of speaking. There were times when I had to stop him in mid-sentence and ask, "Can you define that for me?"

He had an uncanny ability to know all of the guys on the team on a personal level and understand how we operated as individuals, both on and off the ice. He spent so much time listening. I know he wanted to help us become better curlers, but I think he also wanted to help us become better people.

Our team at the end of the 2004–5 season was made up of Mark Nichols, Keith Ryan, Jamie Korab, and me. Keith had struggled throughout the year and I was at a point where I was looking to make a switch. I went to see Toby at his office in St. John's and asked him what he thought I should do.

As usual, he responded to my question with his own question.

"Brad, do you think your team as currently constituted has a chance of winning the Olympic gold medal?"

I told him I didn't think so.

Toby would normally have come back with another question, but that one time he got straight to the point.

"I agree with you," he said. "You need to make a change."

That's how I knew it was the right decision to move on from Keith and ultimately to bring Mike Adam in.

I also talked to Toby about adding a fifth to our team for the first time. By rule, it didn't have to be someone from Newfoundland. We could bring in a curler from anywhere in Canada. The truth is, I already had a name in mind, but I wanted to go through the process with Toby.

We wanted someone who had experience and who could take a little bit of the leadership burden off of me. I was twenty-five and a very good curler who could make a lot of shots. But I had some flaws. I was impatient and temperamental. It would make sense to bring in a veteran, a steady hand, someone who had already experienced the Olympic trials and could contribute a little bit of calm in addition to skill.

There was also an added factor. At one time or another we had beaten most of the top Canadian teams that would be at the trials—but they had beaten us much more often than we had beaten them. If we went up against a Kevin Martin or a Randy Ferbey, there was an intimidation factor because of their reputations. If we could bring in someone who would level that playing field, who was intimidating in his own right, maybe we would stand a better chance of winning.

Toby and I got down to a list of three players. I don't remember who the third was, but I know that Kerry Burtnyk of Manitoba was someone we discussed at length.

But there was one name that stood out—the same one I had started with in my own mind. Russ Howard.

Russ was a guy who had won everything there was to win in curling—except an Olympic medal. He would be the perfect addition, and he would be motivated.

Toby called Russ and put him on speakerphone. We didn't have to twist his arm. He was super excited to have the opportunity to go to the trials and help a young team.

Russ understood that joining us as a fifth was purely a support role. Barring an emergency, he wasn't going to be playing.

Well, that last part wasn't entirely true.

Toby and I had already discussed the possibility that if Mike got off to a slow start, we might want to make a change.

At the beginning of the season, we weren't playing very well. We'd win a couple of games, then we'd lose a couple of games. We made the odd playoff but didn't make any deep runs.

Maybe if Mike had played well and we had won a couple of events, we would have left things as they were. But Mike was struggling, not making shots that he should have, and we decided that it didn't make any sense to have Russ Howard sitting on the bench when a chance to go to the Olympics was on the line.

I talked with Toby and I talked to Mark, and I told them that I thought it was time to bring Russ into the lineup, have him play second and hold the broom.

It was my job to sit down with Mike and let him know that he was going to become our fifth. Obviously he wasn't thrilled, but he handled it as well as anybody could have. He said he would do everything he could to make the team successful. Mike went out of his way to make it easy for me, and we never had to walk on eggshells around him.

That said, it wasn't a simple switch. I'm a skip. Russ is a skip. We had to figure out how we were going to play together. He had to understand what was going to work for me and I had to understand what was going to work for him.

We came to an agreement that I would stay out of his hair during the first four rocks of the end and let him call that part of the game without much input.

But when we got to Mark's shots and my shots, it was my call. Whatever I wanted to play, we were going to play. In the end, I still needed to be able to follow my instincts.

There's a lot of science in the modern game of curling. But sometimes it's not all about the data and analytics.

Sometimes you have to rely on your gut. Sometimes you're comfortable with your draw weight but you're not throwing your hits well. That's when you should play the draw even if the hit is the better option—because you believe in the shot. That kind of decision-making is part of what makes a great skip.

Russ respected the boundaries that we set out. But the flip side was that at the beginning of an end, I had to surrender the control I had enjoyed ever since I started skipping as a teenager.

There were a bunch of times when Russ called for a shot where

I would have called for something different. But we had talked that kind of situation through with Toby and the rest of the team and made the agreement that those would be Russ's decision, so I bit my tongue. At least I knew that I was ceding control to one of the best curlers of all time.

The most impressive part was how Russ handled the back half of those ends.

I was handing off the first four shots to someone with vast experience at the highest level of the sport. He was handing off the last four shots to a twenty-five-year-old who hadn't really achieved a whole lot in the sport other than winning the world junior championship.

Russ had a real air of cockiness about him—cockiness in a good way. When you competed against him in his prime and he used that loud roar to call the sweepers, he was scary.

After Russ joined us, we became a more difficult team to play. There was a newness and freshness in our game. And almost immediately, a lot of things started to break our way.

At one point during that season, I had to make thirteen last rocks in a row to win games that were vital to us getting to the Olympics. Even if you're 85 percent or 90 percent, you're likely going to miss one or two of those. To make all thirteen—and a lot of those were really difficult shots—you know you've got something special going on.

The last event that we played before the trials was in Utica, New York. We went through the round robin undefeated before losing in the quarterfinals. Even though we didn't win, it felt great. We could tell that we were a different team than the one that had started the season.

Just before the trials began in Halifax, there was a story in one of the Winnipeg newspapers where the reporter asked Jeff Stoughton to handicap the field. He said that Kevin Martin was one of the favourites, and of course Alberta's Randy Ferbey. He thought that his own rink was right there.

And then Jeff was asked about our team.

Stoughton said he was surprised we had made what a lot of curling people thought was a desperation move, bringing Russ in at the last minute. And he said we had zero chance of winning.

I got a copy of that article and I put it in my bag before I flew to Halifax, just in case I needed a little added motivation. (I still have that article in my scrapbook at home.)

We felt very much at home playing in the Maritimes, and the crowd at the Metro Centre was behind us from the start. And, by accident, we picked up what became one of our trademarks.

At the Olympic trials, they provided the uniforms. You showed up and they'd give you a box with your jerseys in it. When we opened our box, the jerseys were an unbelievably bright shade of fluorescent orange. We thought it was a joke and we were a little bit embarrassed to put them on. We knew that when we walked out into the rinks for the first time, there were going to be some people giggling.

But then we said, we're the youngest team here. We can get away with it. Let's embrace the orange. Let's own it.

Soon enough we started seeing people in the stands wearing orange shirts. No doubt a lot of them were Newfoundlanders there to support our team. As the week went on, the people in orange shirts were joined by others who were wearing orange garbage bags. Apparently, you couldn't buy an orange T-shirt in Halifax because they were all sold out, so our fans had to get creative.

(The shirts became our standard uniform at the trials. In 2021, as the highest-ranked team, we had our choice of colour, and naturally we chose orange—and won again. At the trials in 2025 we were back in orange, though it wasn't quite so fluorescent.) Our first game was against Glenn Howard's Ontario rink. They were a really good team with a legitimate shot at winning.

We played a great game, but it was close. Going into the last end we were up by one, and I had to draw the four-foot for the win.

I pulled what I like to think of as a "Russ Howard move"—I let the rock go, thought it was light, and called Russ out to help the sweepers (which, truth be told, wouldn't have helped much because Russ was not much of a sweeper).

I started screaming and panicking, and the guys swept it for the first two-thirds of the sheet and then dusted it into the tee line for the win. I remember having a good laugh with Russ about it afterwards.

Getting that first one under our belts, especially coming against Glenn, was really important for our confidence.

I can't overstate Russ's impact during the trials. His experience in that environment was a huge boost for the rest of us. He never looked nervous or out of sorts because he'd seen it all before.

The closest we came to going off the rails was when we lost to Pat Ryan of B.C.—which turned out to be the only game that we dropped that week. We were undefeated in the round robin to that point and playing really well, and Pat's team wasn't one of the stronger ones in the field. It was a game that, on paper, we should have won. But for some reason I started to feel nervous and missed two shots that cost us the win.

In a situation like that, your mind starts working overtime. You start to wonder if things are about to turn against you.

A couple of games later we played B.C.'s Jay Peachey, who hadn't won a game up to that point, and we struggled again.

The game was tied in the last end when I missed my first shot really badly. Jay followed up and made his shot—but he didn't make it perfectly. We had a rock on the back of the button, and if his shot had frozen to it, there would have been no way to get his stone out because of the way the guards were staggered up front. We wouldn't have had a runback or a draw—we wouldn't have had anything.

But fortunately for us, Jay left a little bit of the rock on the high side of the sheet and about an inch exposed. That's all I had to work with.

To reach it I had to play the in-turn, but we hadn't played that side of the ice at all, and if you don't play on a section of ice for a long time it can tighten up and get slower because a layer of frost builds up. And when you're on the side closest to the crowd, heat comes down onto the ice and creates even more of that frost. I didn't have a great read on the ice other than knowing that it was going to be slow.

I remember thinking, *I've just got to give it to the sweepers and let them judge it.* My job was to make sure I got it on the line and threw enough weight to get it there.

When I let the rock go, I remember feeling I had thrown it as well as I possibly could. After that I became a passenger, because Russ was so good at calling the line and the other guys were so good at calling the weight. As the stone got to the hog line, I could see that they were sweeping and then not sweeping, sweeping then not sweeping, which is usually a sign that it was really, really close.

The rock came into the rings and rubbed up against the one that Jay had just thrown.

I couldn't tell if it had rolled off too far for us to get a shot. The guys were looking over the top and I raised my hands, asking, "Who won?"

And then Jamie put his arms up in the air and I knew we had it.

I think that was the greatest shot I had ever made, especially given the stakes, the ice, and the small area I had to play with.

Kevin Martin had just finished up his game on the sheet next to us, and I remember that his lead, Don Bartlett, came over and congratulated me right on the ice, even before I had the chance to shake Jay Peachey's hand. He understood the difficulty of that shot.

Our last game in the round robin was against John Morris. We had already locked up a playoff spot, and the winner of that game would go directly to the final. That game was on a Thursday and the final wasn't happening until Sunday night. We got off to a good start in the game and it never felt like we were in any danger of losing.

All of a sudden, though, my nerves really kicked in. I had trouble sleeping. I had trouble eating. I was in this kind of dark zone where I wanted to stay focused, but I couldn't enjoy anything that was going on around me. All I could think about was that game coming up.

Every morning we would go to a café down the street from our hotel for breakfast—an incredible breakfast—and the owners and staff would treat us really well. I remember walking in there on Friday morning and ordering what I had ordered all week, and I couldn't touch it. I just could not eat.

That happened again at lunch and again at dinner. For two days I barely ate anything. I spent the worst forty-eight hours of my competitive curling career waiting for the final, which ended up being against Manitoba's Jeff Stoughton.

Finally on Sunday the tension broke. I had an appetite again. And once I got out on the ice, it was remarkable how relaxed I felt.

We started the game scoring two in the first end. They followed up and got two right back. We played a great end in the third and got another two—so now it was 4–2 in the fourth and we had an opportunity to steal one, but I'd have to make a perfect shot with my last rock. The throw was just a little bit heavy and a little bit wider than what I wanted, and left Jeff what I thought was a relatively easy shot to score. I felt I had let him off the hook.

When I saw his rock come down the sheet it looked really tight and like it was going to over-curl. By the time it got to the hog line, I knew for sure that Jeff had missed the shot. We stole two to put us up 6–2. And from that position, we were almost guaranteed a win.

For the next six ends, it was all about holding on to the lead, doing everything we could to minimize the amount they could score. In the fifth end, I had a chance for a double that would have held them to one point, but I missed the shot and gave them two, allowing Jeff's team to creep back into the game.

Heading into the last end, we were two up without the hammer. Everybody on our team was just so tight, more wound up than I had ever seen us—Russ included. I know I was feeling the pressure and the stress of the moment.

Jamie's job was to draw into the top of the four-foot to put a rock in a position where Jeff would eventually have to deal with it. Unfortunately, he threw up a guard instead, in the worst possible spot. Jeff added a corner guard, and then we decided to peel off Jamie's rock because it was in such a bad position.

Russ made his two shots, and then Mark missed a peel to take out a rock, which almost never happened. All of a sudden there was a chance that Jeff could score three points and win the game or at least score two to tie it and send it to an extra end.

If Jeff made a perfect hit and roll with his last rock, I would have had to play a very difficult corner freeze around a corner guard.

He threw it really well and his team swept it 90 percent of the way. I knew it was very close. Then Jeff hollered "Whoa!" and called off the sweepers. There was a little panic in his voice. They thought he was going to roll too far after the hit.

We got up there, ready to sweep the rock out of the rings, and got it clear, but then it seemed to turn back just a little bit. I looked over the top and I decided that if the rings were true, it was out by a millimetre or two.

Now, if we hadn't been playing at the Olympic trials and it wasn't the final, there would have been no question in my mind that the rock was out. But with the pressure of the situation, some doubt naturally crept in. What if the measurement of the rings on the ice was off by just a little bit? All it would take was a tiny mistake by the ice maker. What if I was just wishing that it was out?

I usually let Mark or Jamie be the ones to call whether a rock is shot or not, or whether it was in or out of the rings. But I thought I could see white between the rings and the rock, so I made the decision myself. That meant, in a worst-case scenario, we'd be playing an extra end. But if I made my shot, we were going to the Olympics.

I had two options: a corner freeze or a runback.

We went back to that original deal that we had agreed on, where if Russ and I disagreed on one of my shots, I'd be free to follow my instincts.

"What about the freeze?" Russ said.

But I felt more comfortable with the runback. "No, I got it."

Russ got quiet.

"Okay, buddy," he said. "Make 'er."

I put the broom down and threw it.

The feeling was very similar to the one I'd had when I threw that draw earlier in the event against Peachey. Sometimes as a skip, when you let go of the last rock in a pressure situation, it feels like a big sigh of relief.

I was happy with the line. It was just a little bit on the high side and I was waiting and waiting for the stone to curl. Then it made a big move. Russ and I both called on the sweepers, and the guys got on it, just enough to get the back rock out.

I jumped up and down and yelled. My shirt came untucked because I was pumping my arm so much. But as I came down to the other end, I remember Toby saying to me, "Prepare yourself for the extra end."

"I think we've got it," I said.

Toby being the coach he was, and the person he was, knew that his job was to settle me down so we could play that extra end if we had to.

Jeff threw his last shot. You could tell from his body language that he also thought the rock was out. Finally, the measurement confirmed it.

Then the moment sank in. The relief, the joy. The excitement.

We were going to the Olympics.

As you can imagine, there was quite the celebration in Halifax that night.

5

NOVEMBER 16, 2025

The guys on the team had been asking me all that summer of 2025 what my plans were for the next season and beyond that to the next Olympic quadrennial. When we got together for a training camp in Edmonton in September it was time to tell them that I was retiring at the end of the season. After that I'd decide how to let the rest of the curling world know.

It was important to get the timing right around my decision, because once I told the team, they were naturally going to talk to other players and pretty soon everyone was going to find out. It was just a matter of whether I wanted to control the news or let it spread like wildfire.

Our preseason camp was a little longer than usual—seven full days. We practised twice a day and used the rest of the time for workouts and the occasional round of golf. We had just finished our second practice on day four and returned to the rented house we were sharing when I decided the time was right to let the guys know that this was going to be my last year.

I held up pretty well at the start. But then I saw Mark's eyes getting watery and red and I looked over at Geoff and he was the same. That's when I broke down.

"Guys," I said, trying to lighten the mood, "let's talk about something else for a while."

Breaking the news went as well as I ever could have hoped. The guys were very kind and empathetic. They were more worried about me than about themselves. No one was talking about what the season was going to be like or what they were going to do in the future.

After a couple of hours, Brendan, Adam Casey, and our coach, Jeff Hoffart, left, so it was just me and Mark and Geoff. The three of us had been together for a long time. We sat up late into the night and shared some stories.

The next morning we were all back to telling jokes, and the remaining days of the camp were so much fun. A weight had been lifted off my shoulders.

Kevin Martin was around the rink that week and had been watching us practise. He wouldn't know that I was retiring until the public announcement came out later, but one day, after I had told the team, he came up to me and said: "I noticed you were different out there today. You were so much looser than I'm used to seeing you on the ice."

His words stuck with me. It must have been so obvious. Kevin had picked it up just from seeing me on the ice.

Now it was time to go public.

Krista thought that I owed our great, supportive fan base more than just a written statement. It was her idea to record a video.

We tried to do it ourselves. I wrote a script—and Krista hated it. I wrote another one—and she hated that one as well. We finally agreed on the words, but when we tried to film it, we couldn't get it to look the way we wanted. It was time to bring in the professionals. I reached out to a friend of a friend who is in the marketing business and who could take care of the filming. They also had a writer on hand who helped me with the script.

The crew had to sign NDAs so the news wouldn't leak out. The video was supposed to be one take, five minutes. But I couldn't get through the filming without breaking down. This surprised me because I was so content and so happy with the decision I'd made and was excited about what was going to happen after my career is done. I thought I was past all the tears. But as soon as I started talking about the team, it was a little overwhelming.

When we finally got a version of the video that we liked, we released it on the internet.

And then, watching the video, Krista and I went through all the emotions again, crying together and hugging.

Our daughter Marissa was sitting at the table eating her dinner, and she didn't move. She just kept eating like nothing unusual was happening while the two of us were sobbing behind her.

That's Marissa . . .

Then the messages started coming in. So many of them. People mentioned that they'd cried watching the video. "You're the best ever." "I wish you weren't quitting." "Have no idea what I'm going to do now that you've retired."

I was pretty overwhelmed.

I didn't sleep well that night, but I woke up the next morning feeling a huge sense of relief.

Now everybody knew, and I could move on.

I am curious to see how the new, relaxed me is going to perform in the final season.

When I look back over the course of my career, the only period where I felt that I was playing carefree was at the 2017 world championships. We had just won our first Brier and we were the best team in the world by a wide margin. There was no pressure on our backs and we absolutely destroyed the field.

I'd love to feel like that again. No pressure. No expectations. But I also know that to play at a high level I have to be sharp and focused. I've got to find a way to make sure that I have that intensity on the ice.

The season has been disappointing so far. Our team really hasn't come together yet. Practices have been good. We're throwing really well and making a ton of shots. But in games we are just not matching up. It's like Tiger Woods used to say: "We're great on the range, but we're not making the shots on the golf course."

I admit that my motivation has been a little hit-and-miss. There are some games where I really want to be there and really want to play great. And then there are other games where I feel a level of indifference. Winning and losing just doesn't seem to matter as much to me as it did even a few years ago. I still want to play well, but as much as I want to give it, there are days when it doesn't feel like there's much gas left in the tank.

It's incredibly frustrating. I want to be good, I want to be motivated, but sometimes it's just not there.

I've also been spending a lot of time talking to curling fans across the country. Ever since I announced my retirement, people have been coming up to me everywhere I go to share their stories, telling me how much they appreciate what I've accomplished. A lot of them have tears in their eyes.

That's been a bit hard to process. I don't want to get emotional anymore. I've dealt with that since last summer. It's nice to know that people care so much, but it's also difficult knowing I made someone cry.

The last thing I wanted for the final season was for it to turn into a "farewell tour." I want to compete. I want people to cheer for us because we're winning, not because it is the last time they're going to see us play.

The crowds have been amazing. When we played Brad Jacobs in Calgary at the PointsBet Invitational, you could draw a line through the building. On the left side, it was empty. And on the right side, next to the sheet where we were playing, it was full. Every single seat.

I feel a bit guilty knowing that 90 percent of the crowd is there to see us, but it's also pretty cool. After every game, I have been trying to spend as much time with the fans as possible, signing autographs and having pictures taken.

I know I made the right decision. No second thoughts. No regrets. I'm going to enjoy this final season as much as I can and embrace the moment. I've found that when I make a great shot or we win a game, I'm looking around a little bit more than usual and thinking, This might be the last time.

I'm hoping that as the year goes on, the emotional part gets a little less intense. But there's one week of our schedule that is going to be a huge test in that respect. I know the Brier at home in St. John's is going to be a shit show, and there's nothing I can do about that.

♣

I should talk about the physical challenges I have been facing this year. Though no one outside of our team knows it, this has been a gruelling season for me.

In October, a couple of weeks after I made the retirement announcement, we were playing at the PointsBet at the Olympic Park in Calgary.

The day before the event started, we played a round of golf and then had a really good practice on the ice. When I got out of bed the next morning, my back was pretty tight. I decided to go down to the hot tub and try to loosen it up, because we had two practices scheduled and then our first game the next day.

As I was walking towards the hot tub, my steps became shorter and shorter until I got halfway down the hall and couldn't walk at all. My back was so tight that I literally couldn't move.

I had never in my life experienced anything like it.

I called our coach, Jeff Hoffart, but he couldn't help me on his own so he called the other guys. Mark and Geoff arrived, and it took all three of them to carry me down the hall and into the hot tub.

I wasn't getting a ton of relief, though, so Jeff made appointments for me with a local physiotherapist and a doctor. The guys helped me back up to my room, I was able to get changed, and then we headed down to the car.

I collapsed in the parking lot with another back spasm. I wound up lying face down on the pavement, unable to move.

It was a scary moment.

I remember thinking, What the hell am I doing? So this is where I am in my career, face down in a parking lot, screaming in pain, worrying about who is going to see me. It was disheartening, to say the least.

Geoff tried to hold me up, and as I collapsed again, I ended up hurting his back. It took ten minutes for the spasm to ease off to the point where Geoff, Mark, and Jeff could lift me into the car.

They finally got me to the clinic and I was given painkillers and muscle relaxants. The only reason I got through that week was because we were right across the street from the Olympic Park, where we had access to doctors, physiotherapists, chiropractors, and osteopaths.

I went through so much dry needling during those days that I felt like a pincushion, but at least I was able to play—though in a compromised and heavily medicated state. I couldn't execute my normal delivery because I was so tight. I had to change my approach just to get out of the hack.

I guess this is the reality of this late stage in my career, dealing with nagging back as well as hip, knee, and neck injuries that have piled up over the years. You don't have to worry about that stuff when you're twenty or twenty-five years old. But at forty-five, it's different—it's more like, what kind of Band-Aid do I need to put on to get me through the next game? These days I'm never really playing at 100 percent. I'm always at least a little bit hurt.

I didn't miss a game in Calgary, but I should have missed a few. The reason I kept going was that I didn't want to attract any more attention. We finished 2–2 and didn't make the playoff.

One of the advantages of not living and dying with the results of every game at this stage of my career is that I've been able to relax and enjoy myself a bit more outside of the sport. For instance, I'm not sure if even a year ago I would have taken time in the middle of the season to watch a bunch of baseball games.

We were playing an event in Switzerland in October when the Toronto Blue Jays were in the World Series. I'm a big baseball fan—I watched probably a hundred games during the season and went to seven or eight in person, so there was no way I was going to miss the playoffs. And if I had known the Jays were going to go that far, we wouldn't have gone to Switzerland in the first place.

The problem was that with the time difference, the games didn't start until one in the morning local time.

We figured out a routine. We'd go to bed at six and set the alarm for shortly before one. In theory, we'd get our seven hours of sleep. Then we got up and watched the game, which would end around five.

Our first game of the playoffs was at 8 a.m. We tried to grab another half-hour of sleep and then we'd start with our warm up. Like all Blue Jays fans after watching four hours of playoff baseball, we were emotionally drained and then we had to go out and perform.

We curled terribly—absolutely terribly. It's no surprise that we lost. But it was the Jays in the World Series and it meant so much to us to be able to watch history that we had to sacrifice something.

The curling was the sacrifice.

Now, there's a sentence I don't think I could have spoken when I was younger.

Another of the real joys I have experienced this year is being able to see my girls play. I guess it's a bit of a preview of what my life will be like after I retire as a player and have more time to spend with them during the season.

I love seeing how they deal with different competitive situations.

Marissa was invited to take part in an event in Nisku, Alberta, in the fall of 2025, at the same time as I was playing there at the Co-op Tour Challenge, and there was a chance that if both our teams had made the final, she and I would have been on the ice at the same time.

We started that event pretty well and I began to think that if we did reach the final, I was going to wind up paying more attention to Marissa's game than to my own. That's the point I'm at in my life right now. In the end we didn't get that far, so I could fully concentrate on Marissa's game. She ended up losing a heartbreaker in a shootout.

Marissa was so cool and calm and collected. She's a fourteen-year-old girl, and I'm not sure that, as a forty-five-year-old man, I would've handled that defeat as well as she did.

I'm proud that both of my girls respect the etiquette of the game. They're not spoiled brats and they're not sore losers. They go about it the right way. And I know that they get that from their mother—because I was definitely a sore loser when I was their age.

I've been thinking a lot about my daughters and what is going to happen down the road. I think that I enjoy simply watching Hayley and Marissa more than I would coaching them, because when you're a coach you've got skin in the game. As a parent, you can focus on your own kid and how they're performing, but as a coach, you've got to think about the whole team. I don't know if that's in my future.

But following my girls and supporting them certainly will be. I've missed a lot of their games in the past and even this year. Hayley played an event in Ottawa that I couldn't even stream because I was in Switzerland. There are a lot of conflicts during the season where I end up having to record their games and watch them later.

When I'm in the rink, I'm a pretty quiet curling parent. I get a little frustrated when they make a bad decision on the ice, but I understand that they're still learning and obviously they don't have the experience that I do.

After a game, I try not to tell them if they made a bad call. I wait for them to ask me, and then I'll say that maybe I would have played something a little different and I'll explain why.

I think we've got a really good learning dynamic. I don't want to put pressure on them. I've never pushed them to curl—if anything, I pushed them away from competitive curling—but they found the love for the game on their own. I don't want them to feel like they have to play. Part of me almost wishes that they could just curl for fun, for recreation, for the love of the game. Because I know with their last name, they are going to attract extra attention and face extra pressure.

There was a story written about Marissa playing in Nisku. And Sportsnet is sending a crew to St. John's to do a story about me but they are also interviewing the girls. I'm a little nervous about how they're going to handle that.

I remember a number of years ago when we did a marketing piece for one of our sponsors, Kubota. They arranged to interview Marissa and Hayley, who were probably eight and twelve at the time. The interviewer started to ask Hayley questions, and she didn't know how to answer. Then she got really nervous, she got emotional, and she started to cry. It broke my heart to see that. I never want to put her in that position.

I don't envy the girls attracting the attention that will come their way if they decide to keep curling competitively, especially knowing that given the choice, I avoided it as much as possible.

So far, they're handling it really well.

Now we are heading into the Olympic trials in Halifax.

I have a lot of confidence that I'm going to be able to play well, even though I haven't been very good so far this year. Leading the team and getting the most out of them is just as important, and I admit that's also something I haven't done as well as I should have.

I'm motivated by this one last chance to have the kind of experience we had in 2006.

The guys have talked about Beijing, and how, despite the pandemic, it was still an Olympics and it was great, but it paled in comparison to the Games in Italy. It would be great for Geoff and

Brendan and Mark and me to be able to experience what Mark and I did in Turin.

Winning another medal would be fantastic, but it would be just as important to have our families there, to play in front of a big crowd, explore the city, and enjoy all that the Olympics has to offer—all the things we didn't get to do in Beijing.

And if we don't make it? If we don't win the trials?

I think I would still be okay with that.

If you'd asked me that question in the past, I would have given you a different answer. Winning meant everything to me. I knew I would be devastated if I didn't make it.

But I'm in a place now where it's still a big thing—but I know it's not the only thing.

6

TURIN, 2006

The first stage of our Olympic orientation began the morning after winning the trials in Halifax. We were still hungover from celebrating the night before, so I'm not sure the representatives of the Canadian Olympic Committee had our full attention.

We were told when we were going to leave for Italy, what the Olympic Village was going to be like, what the schedule would be throughout the week, who would be going with us. They asked us if there was anything special that the team was going to need over there. I remember I asked them for a case of root beer. That was my only special request.

It wasn't until I got home to Newfoundland that I started to realize how my life was about to change. I had a bunch of media requests. The premier wanted us to visit him in his office. Members of the provincial House of Assembly and federal members of Parliament reached out. Our curling club wanted to do all kinds of things with us.

It was the middle of December, so there was also Christmas coming up and all the chaos that comes with that. We thought that at some point it might be a good idea for our team to get together somewhere quiet and practise on our own.

In January, Russ suggested that we all go to his family cottage near Midland, Ontario. The Penetanguishene Curling Club was there. It sounded like a great idea.

We landed in Toronto in the middle of what turned out to be one of the worst snowstorms of the winter. The drive to Midland that was supposed to be only a couple of hours wound up taking closer to seven. It felt like it took forever.

When we finally got to Russ's cabin, he discovered he didn't have his keys. It also turned out that the place wasn't really properly winterized.

The only hotel we could find in the area was a rundown, dingy Super 8—a two out of ten on the quality scale. That's where we ended up staying.

To top things off, I got an infected tooth. It wasn't the best situation, but we at least got a bit of practice in.

On February 9, 2006, the day before the opening ceremony, we flew to Turin. We walked into the Olympic Village for the first time and I remember that the maintenance team was still laying sod. The preparations for the Games were coming down to the wire.

The security was especially tight because this was after 9/11 and because not long before, a Danish magazine had published a series of cartoons that had upset much of the Muslim world and the Danish team had received threats. We had to go through checkpoint after checkpoint to enter and exit the village and the venues.

Once we got inside the village, the atmosphere was much more relaxed and very cool. We ran into the Canadian women's hockey team and we ended up becoming good friends with them—Mike Adam actually dated one of the players for a while after the Games. The first time we saw a medal close up was when the women won their gold four days before our final. I remember holding the medal and thinking, *I want one of these really bad.*

The opening ceremony was a lot of fun, though it wasn't quite as glamorous as the part you see on TV. They herded all the athletes into an arena where we sat for hours until our country was called to file into the stadium. We filled that time telling stories and laughing and singing.

When we finally got the cue to start walking, I could feel the adrenaline filling my body. As we entered the Stadio Olimpico, we heard the roar from the crowd, and that's when it really dawned on us that we were part of the Olympics. It was one of the best moments of my career.

The ceremony was long but great. They had a Ferrari F1 car come out and do donuts on the stage, and Luciano Pavarotti sang. It was an amazing show. There were also incredible fireworks. It all culminated with the lighting of the Olympic cauldron.

By the time we got back to the village it was late at night, and we shut it down because first thing the next morning we were leaving for Pinerolo, a cute little town about an hour's drive from Turin, where the curling competition would take place.

Curling Canada had rented the top two floors of an apartment building in Pinerolo so we wouldn't have to commute back and forth to Turin every day. It was a great set-up for us, but not so great for the families and friends of the team, who found out when they arrived that the hotel rooms they thought they had booked had been handed over to someone else.

They found rooms in another place, not very nice and way out of the way, too far to walk to the venue where we were going to be competing, and the local public transit shut down at night before our games were finished. My dad finally found a bus driver who the families paid to pick them up each night.

Toby had his wife and two kids with him and Russ had his wife and two kids. As a husband and father, you obviously want to make sure your family is taken care of, so those two wound up carrying an extra burden in addition to whatever was happening on the ice. But they kept that from the rest of us so we wouldn't be distracted.

There was also the added complication that no one where the families were staying spoke English, which did have one funny consequence. My dad was unknowingly buying alcohol-free beer at the bar for the first few days before someone finally pointed it out to him. The placebo effect seemed to have worked pretty well, though, because there had apparently been times at the bar when he started speaking fluent Italian.

Curling at the Olympics is a completely different beast than what we were used to back home. From day one I could tell that Russ was out of his element, unsettled by the magnitude of the Games. He had accomplished everything you could in curling, but he had never been to the Olympics, and it was different in so many ways.

For instance, the first time we left the athletes' village, Russ didn't bother to bring his accreditation with him. At the trials, at the Brier, you were given a credential, but if you were Russ Howard no one ever asked to see it. Everyone knew who you were. You could walk around the building like you owned the place. Russ did that, I did that. It's just the way it was.

But at the Olympics, Russ Howard was just an athlete like everybody else. During the Games, you had to show your credentials every place you went—you even had to be accredited to get into a washroom. That was a completely different world for Russ, and for all of us. He was unsettled by it, I think, and it took away some of his confidence.

When I was nine months old. I loved the suit. (Courtesy of the author.)

Krista and I on our wedding day in 2006. (Courtesy of the author.)

Krista and I in Kingston, ON, when I received my MBA from Queen's University. (Courtesy of the author.)

First time meeting Russ Howard, along with my sister, Natasha. Russ presented me with the All-Star Skip award at the 2000 Canadian Junior Curling Championship in Moncton, NB. (Courtesy of the author.)

Krista and I at the Brier Patch at the 2003 Nokia Brier in Halifax, NS. (Courtesy of the author.)

Jack MacDuff and I playing a fundraising game before the 2001 World Junior Curling Championships. (Courtesy of the author.)

Our team posting the messages from the school kids in our locker room at the 2006 Winter Olympics in Torino, Italy. (Courtesy of the author.)

My family after the final shot in the Bronze Medal game at the 2022 Winter Olympics in Beijing, China. (Courtesy of the author.)

Our team with my friend, Bob Cole, during an intermission at the Canada vs. Germany game at the 2006 Winter Olympics in Torino, Italy. (Courtesy of the author.)

Marissa pretending she won an Olympic Gold Medal . . . too cute!
(Courtesy of the author.)

One of our first family curling outings with my daughters and nephews.
(Courtesy of the author.)

Hayley at her first Brier in 2007, and then when we played the provincial mixed doubles championships together. (Courtesy of the author.)

I love being in the outdoors and kayaking at our cabin. (Courtesy of the author.)

Getting to play an event in the Red Square in Moscow, Russia, was quite an experience. (Courtesy of the author.)

Mom, Dad, and I after our first Brier win in St. John's in 2017. They were a big part of making it happen. (Courtesy of the author.)

Me handing the Tankard trophy to the crowd in the patch after our Brier win in St. John's. (Courtesy of the Danielle Inglis/Curling Canada.)

At the trials we'd been happy to follow Russ's lead and lean into his experience, but in Italy he was travelling the same learning curve that we were as twenty-four- and twenty-five-year-olds.

When we got on the ice for our first practice session, we realized immediately that the conditions weren't going to be ideal, the way they had been during the trials. We were used to ice that was running fourteen, fifteen seconds—quick ice with lots of curl where it was easy to get a feel for draw weight. (Most top curling teams, in order to get a sense of the speed of the ice, will time a shot with a stopwatch. They'll start the timer when the rock is released from the first hog line and stop it when it hits the other line. Typically, it'll take anywhere from fourteen to fifteen and a half seconds for that rock to get down the ice. That difference in the half seconds can mean anywhere from four to six feet. So if you're trying to throw a fourteen-and-a-half-second shot, and it ends up fourteen seconds, it's probably going to be four feet heavier, because it took less time to travel between the hog lines, which mean it's moving faster.) That's definitely the way Russ liked it, the way it would be at a Brier. In Pinerolo it was more like thirteen, maybe thirteen and a half—which doesn't sound like much, but it has a completely different feel.

Russ was especially frustrated by the ice because those conditions were not at all conducive to the way he liked to play. He started to talk about all the things that were wrong with the event. The ice wasn't curling as much. It wasn't as quick as we wanted. He was out of sorts, and that continued for our first few games and it started feeding through the rest of our team.

Our first game was against Germany. We won 10–5, but it wasn't nearly as comfortable as that score would suggest. We kind of scraped through.

In our second game, we were in against Peja Lindholm from Sweden, a very good team. I had a chance to draw to the four-foot for the win, a pretty straightforward shot. When the rock reached the top of the rings, the guys were just cleaning it. It looked like it was right at the tee line. And then at the top of the twelve-foot, the rock picked on a little stone on the ice and ended up coming six inches short of what we needed.

That was a shock. You get picks all the time in curling, but to have one that late in the shot—let alone on a potential last shot—and that drastic is very, very rare. We were all pretty devastated by the loss.

It reached the point where we just had to stop complaining about the ice and the rocks and anything else that wasn't perfect.

Leading up to Turin, we had a talk with Marnie McBean, the great Canadian rower and Olympian. To this day, I will never forget her number one piece of advice to us: "Suck it up, princess." What she meant was that when things weren't going our way, we had to remember that we were at the Olympics and that there were a lot worse places we could be.

To be honest I can't remember who called the team meeting—it was probably Toby—but when we got together, he didn't take the lead. He always liked to deal with us one-on-one, planting seeds and allowing us to come together on our own.

Russ acknowledged that the ice was still an issue for him. But it came back to what Marnie had told us: "Suck it up." The conditions weren't great and there were a lot of frustrations on and off the ice, but we were at the Olympics, we knew we were the best team there, and we had to find a way to win.

I took on a little bit more of a leadership role at that point. I was starting to feel pretty comfortable in the Olympic environment and I was throwing the rock really well. I was ready to take some of the pressure off Russ and put it on myself.

I'd like to take a moment to offer a different side of Russ. He is actually a pretty easygoing guy. Considering that he was a fifty-year-old dealing with a bunch of much younger guys, he did a great job fitting in with our team.

Our apartment in Pinerolo was on the top floor of one of the tallest buildings in the town. Jamie and I were on one side of the hall and Russ, Mark, and Mike were on the other side. One day I walked over to their rooms and I could hear some laughter. I was wondering, what the hell were these guys up to? And then I saw the four of them out on the balcony, firing paper airplanes to see how far they would go.

So, pretty harmless stuff. But then Russ had the idea that it would be fun to set the paper airplanes on fire. That's when I ducked out.

But when I think about it now, it was great that Russ was out there doing the stupid shit that twenty-year-olds do. And not just doing it but instigating it.

Later that week we played the home team, Italy, skipped by Joël Retornaz, who turned out to be an impressive player (although back then he did not have a good team, and he wasn't the player he is today). The crowd was like a soccer crowd, cheering for their guys and against us. They were loud. They were heckling. They booed our made shots and cheered our misses. It was the complete opposite of what a curling crowd back home would do.

But I have to admit that part of me really enjoyed it. It was the most intense atmosphere I have ever played in and it was fun, even if we were looked at as the bad guys. I wish we could get that kind of reaction more often.

We got off to a terrible start, fell way behind early, fought back, and ultimately lost. That left us 4–3 in the round robin and on the brink of being eliminated from the playoffs and losing any chance of winning an Olympic medal.

Mark was really struggling. He just wasn't playing with his normal confidence. His timing wasn't quite right, and he wasn't throwing his heavy shots, the peels and the runbacks, the way he normally did—which was as hard as anybody in the world.

The organizers had made available a three-sheet curling club right next to the main venue where we could practise. The ice wasn't great over there, but we needed to use it to allow Mark to try to get his feel back. He was still missing one runback after another and was only throwing seven and a half seconds, which was fairly hard for most people but nowhere near normal Mark Nichols speed.

Finally I said, "Mark, just fucking throw it. Just whip it down there."

He threw one at around six-two, which was more like it, and . . . boom, boom . . . he made the runback. We set it up again and he threw another stone. Boom. He made the shot. He threw six, seven, eight rocks and he made every single one of them. I could sense him starting to get excited.

It was a cool moment. Something had clicked for him. He had his timing back. You could sense his surge in confidence.

I walked off the ice and said to Jim Waite, our team lead, "I think we just won the Olympics."

I know that sounds a bit cocky. But I knew that if Mark was going good and he was making his shots, my shots were going to be easier, and our chances would be so much better.

Mark wound up being our MVP in the playoffs. He averaged 96 percent in the semifinal and final.

Amid all of that tension, there was one funny moment that helped to lighten our mood.

At the Olympics, every team has its own dressing room. We liked to get there well before our start time to shoot the shit. There were pictures and posters and letters from kids back home up on the wall to provide some inspiration.

We had just come off that loss to Italy, and Toby was in the dressing room getting ready to go out and get his bench set up. He was wearing his tight spandexy long johns and his shirt, and then he put his jacket on, put his stopwatch around his neck, grabbed his bag, and set out for the arena.

The only thing he forgot were his pants. And let's just say Toby's body type was not conducive to spandex.

I kind of elbowed Mark, and Mark elbowed Jamie, and Jamie elbowed Russ. Russ was about to say something, and then he looked at us and caught on—let's just let Toby go out and see what happens.

He walked out of the dressing room and we all burst out laughing, waiting for him to figure it out.

Toby must have been out there for four or five minutes, before he realized what he'd done.

"You bunch of bastards," he said when he came back to the dressing room. We were almost rolling on the floor.

Looking back, there's a part of me that wonders if Toby did that on purpose just to lighten the mood. That would be typical of him. He knew we needed that little bit of levity at a point when we were taking things so seriously, and he sure provided it for us.

Fortunately, our next game was against New Zealand, which was not a strong team. That win got us to 5–3. And then in our final round-robin game we played Pete Fenson and his rink from the United States. Pete's team was 6–2 and had already locked up a spot in the playoffs. We knew from playing them in the Slams that they were certainly capable of beating us.

That week, a stomach bug was circulating among the Canadian curling contingent. We had so far managed to avoid it. But the morning of the U.S. game, Jamie woke up ill.

Our coaches and doctors went into his room to check him over. When they came out, they told us he wasn't going to be playing.

You can imagine how that news landed.

Mike Adam was going to have to step in after months of being on the outside as our fifth man. When we had replaced him with Russ, Mike didn't whine or complain. He didn't take the team down. He was such a professional about it.

Now, all of a sudden, we needed him to perform in a must-win game at the Olympics, and he rose to the occasion. Mike was great that day. He curled 88 percent and set us up really well.

It was a scrappy game where we ended up having to steal two in the ninth end to take control. The way it played out, the way Mike filled in for Jamie, we started to feel like maybe this might be our week after all.

There was one more hurdle we had to get over.

We had a day off between that last round-robin game and the semifinal—a rematch against Pete Fenson. And that's when I started to feel a little off—I threw up, and I had diarrhea—all of the symptoms of the stomach bug. It was late at night when I called Toby and Jim Waite. They brought along Dr. Bob McCormack, who gave me a pill to calm down my gut. I got a little sleep, but I woke up the next morning feeling drained, knowing that I had to play a game that could get us into the Olympic final.

Thank God the adrenaline eventually kicked in and I could forget about the night before.

It was a close game against the Americans, but we played really well, and we finally blew it open by scoring five in the ninth end.

I will always remember my last shot in that game. At that point we were only up by one with the hammer, and I could see maybe two inches of the shot rock that we had to pick out. It was one of those shots where the moment you let it go, you know it's made. I was so confident that as soon as it left my hand I was thinking, *How am I going to celebrate this?* That's how well I threw it. By the time it was halfway to the house I was telling myself, *Don't go crazy here, just relax.*

I wound up doing the Statue of Liberty, lifting my hand up in the air. (There are a couple of pictures of that moment, including one that I have framed in my basement along with the team jacket I wore that day.) We had just guaranteed ourselves an Olympic medal, but I didn't want to go overboard because there was still work to be done.

We did in fact celebrate a little that night. With an off-day before the final, we decided to head back to the Olympic Village in Turin. They had an internet café there where we could reconnect with the world. To that point, we had done a pretty good job of cutting ourselves off from any news from home.

Once we had checked in, we figured that we could go to see a hockey game or some speed skating and distract ourselves for a while.

Jamie was by far the most tech-savvy guy in our group, and when we got to the internet café, he was the first one to log on to a computer, ready to go. His first stop was the St. John's *Telegram* website. I'll never forget his reaction.

"Holy shit, boys! They're closing the schools."

The front-page story was about Premier Danny Williams announcing that schools across Newfoundland and Labrador would be closed so that everyone could watch our gold medal game. There was no hiding now. If we fell on our face, everybody at home was going to see it.

I didn't really enjoy the rest of that day and I didn't sleep much at all that night. It felt like I only closed my eyes for an hour or so. But I woke up the next morning revived and ready to get the game going.

Our opponent in the gold medal game was Markku Uusipaavalniemi from Finland. His team was a real surprise at those Olympics. They finished first in the round robin and then beat David Murdoch from Great Britain in their semifinal.

I had always been impressed by Markku. He played incredibly well during the round robin and really carried his team. But I knew that if we could apply some pressure and put him in some tough spots, we were going to win. On the flip side, if we left him with easy shots, he was going to make them. He was that good a player.

We started off slowly, giving up a two, and then we got a two back, and all of a sudden I felt like I was in the rhythm of the game and the nerves went away.

Once we started to apply some pressure, the game turned our way. I could see that Markku was nervous. The Finnish team was making some tight calls and I started to feel a little better about our chances. We got up by a couple of points and then they got one back in the fifth. That left us up 4–3 with the hammer in the sixth—a really good position.

We didn't play our best end in the sixth and the Finns were applying a little pressure on us, putting one rock behind a couple of guards. Mark tried a double peel on the front rocks and missed by just a hair. He ended up hitting one guard close to the nose, running it into the other, and then that guard ran back and took out the Finland rock. It wasn't the shot we intended but it worked out better than it should have.

That left us with three rocks in the rings and Finland none. Markku still had an out, but he didn't execute his shot very well. I made my shot, but not as perfectly as I wanted, leaving Markku a chance with his final rock to hit and roll in and eliminate our four.

The second he let the rock go, Russ said to me, "This is tight. It looks like it's going to hit the guard."

I had to keep my head in the game and be ready to make whatever shot I was going to have to make. I couldn't assume he was going to fail.

"No, it's going to get by," I said.

"It's hitting the guard," Russ said.

He was right.

When it hit, Russ got up to sweep. The rock stopped, and I looked around and I can remember actually counting on my hand—one finger went up, two fingers went up, three, four, and then all of a sudden my thumb—and then I had to go to my other hand. We were lying six because Markku had pushed another one of the rocks into the rings with his shot. I would be drawing for seven with my last shot. We were already up by one.

The game was effectively over. We had just won the Olympic gold medal. The rule was that you have to finish at least eight ends to complete a game, but that wasn't going to change anything now.

"Just draw the button," Russ said.

"No, I can't do that."

"Why not?"

"I don't want to over-curl and bump in their rock. If I don't throw this rock, we win the Olympics."

That's what was going through my head. The rock that I was worried about bumping wasn't really in play at all—at least at our level. But I kept thinking, if their rock somehow got into the rings, the game would be on again.

I ended up trying to draw away from that rock. I got down into the hack and tried to go through my usual routine to settle my body because my heart rate was so high. But for a change it wasn't stress or anxiety that I was feeling—it was joy.

I tried to throw the rock a little softer than I normally would, but as soon as I let go, I could see our two sweepers back off.

They stayed close to the stone the whole way down and it ended up sliding just through the rings. But we still got our six, we were up by seven, and it was just a matter of playing out the game.

It was so awkward playing those last two ends. We knew we weren't going to lose. There was no realistic way that could happen.

But when you're in the moment, with lots of time to think about it, you come up with all kinds of scenarios. *Oh my God, if we somehow lose this, this is going to be the biggest collapse, not only in curling history but in sports history. I've got to stay focused. I've got to stay intense. I can't allow myself to take a victory lap or a rest.*

Mentally I was trying to keep myself in the game as much as I could. There was an internal dialogue going: *Stay in this, Brad. Do not let yourself think too far ahead.* At the same time, the rational part of my brain was telling me that it was over.

I fought with myself for half an hour. And then finally, when we played the last shot in the eighth, and the game really was over, the feeling I had was more relief than excitement. The journey, the stress, the anxiety was done.

Before I played the last shot I looked over to our bench and got Mike Adam's attention.

"Can you get my phone?"

He knew why I was asking. I had to call my mom.

♣

When we got to the Olympic trials, I had made the decision that I didn't want anyone outside of our team to know about Mom's cancer battle—no media, no other curlers. We weren't going to tell anyone. It was great that she was able to be there and cheer us on.

And then on the Saturday, the day before the final, we had some interviews scheduled and Robin Short, the columnist for the St. John's

Telegram, started asking me questions about my mom. I think my dad must have let it slip to him. I wasn't going to lie, so it became a bit of a story leading up to the final.

When I got home from the trials, my priority was to find a way for Mom to get to Italy. I wanted her to be able to share the moment because she had been such a big part of my getting there.

We worked with the Canadian Olympic Committee and Curling Canada to find a solution. She was still in the middle of her treatments, but we put a good plan in place and I was confident it would work out.

A week before the Olympics, Mom had a small setback, and her doctors advised her it wasn't a good idea to travel. (Given all the hassles our families and friends ended up having to go through in Italy, in hindsight the trip would have been way too hard on her.)

What I didn't know during the Games was that Mom had another setback and had been in the hospital for a few days. My family actually snuck her in with a hoodie over her head so that the news wouldn't get out and back to me. The CBC did learn that she had been admitted, but opted not to report it.

When I called home after the last game of the round robin the way I always did, she didn't answer.

I thought that was strange. She must have been watching the game. Why wasn't she answering the phone?

I mentioned it to Krista and Dad (who had travelled to Turin), and both they and Toby told me she must have been busy. There were a lot of people in the house. Maybe she didn't hear the phone. And there was the time difference—we were four and a half hours ahead of Newfoundland. I knew the cancer treatments made Mom tired, so I figured she might have been sleeping.

The same thing happened after the semifinal. I called home and didn't get an answer. The same excuses. Three days had passed and I hadn't had a chance to talk to Mom. It was frustrating, but part of me pushed it aside and figured that what Dad and Krista and Toby were telling me was true. I didn't let myself think that they were trying to manage me. (It wasn't until I got home that I learned everything that had been going on with Mom during the Olympics. There were several times over the course of my career when my family kept things from me to allow me to stay focused. I never liked it, and I would get upset by it, but that was their way of supporting me and supporting our team.)

Mom got out of the hospital on the morning of the final. There were friends and family at the house to look after her and to watch the game with her. The CBC even sent a camera to the house to record her reaction.

After I threw that final rock, our team got together and hugged, and then I waved at Mike and he tossed me the phone.

I thought Mom had to be watching now. She had to be home.

But I still didn't get an answer.

And this is a story that tells you everything you need to know about Newfoundland.

The moment we won the gold medal, a random lady from Badger, in the central part of the province, called the house to congratulate our family. We didn't know her at all and I don't know how she got the number. Maybe just from the phone book.

The lady kept talking and she was very nice and Mom didn't want to hang up on her.

In Italy, they were pulling me aside to do an interview with Bruce Rennie on the CBC broadcast. And I looked into the camera and said, "Mom, pick up the phone."

That's when Mom said goodbye to the lady from Badger, and my call finally went through.

When I heard her voice finally, I broke down crying on national television. (The CBC has footage of Mom's end of the call. When we watch it together now, it's pretty emotional.) Bruce asked me what was said in the call, and that's when I called myself a "sook." I didn't realize that nobody outside of Newfoundland knew what that meant.

At home, it means you're a bit of a crybaby. I had to explain the word to mainlanders for months after. And the truth is, I am a bit of a mama's boy—so much so that when I was still living in my parents' house, I wouldn't go to bed at night until I got a kiss on the forehead from my mother. Now, when we visit her or she comes by our house, we don't leave without her doing the same thing.

Part of me was ready to get on a plane and go straight home to Newfoundland to see Mom. But we had to stay another night to get our medals and then the night after that was the closing ceremony.

After the game, we went back to a local restaurant that had looked after us during the time we were in Pinerolo. There, a very small, intimate group of family and friends enjoyed a fun night of drinking, telling stories, celebrating. There were lots of hugs, there was dancing. It was a great party.

The medal ceremony was going to be held in Turin. We headed back to the athletes' village and went to watch some speed skating and saw Clara Hughes put on an incredible medal-winning performance.

Then it was time to go to the medal ceremony. That was one scary ride, literally. There were three police cars in front of our bus and another three behind it, plus a motorcycle escort. We were going down one-way streets the wrong way with sirens blaring, we were driving up on the curbs. It was a wild trip before we finally pulled into the medals plaza and made the short walk to the stage.

As we were walking, my cellphone rang. The voice on the other end said, "Is Brad Gushue there, please?"

"Speaking."

He introduced himself as the assistant to Stephen Harper, the prime minister of Canada. "Can you please hold for a minute?"

In a few seconds the prime minister came on the line. He was newly elected then and, as it turned out, he was a big curling fan and a supporter of our team. We had a really good conversation. He was super kind, and super knowledgeable about the sport. He had watched a lot of the matches and talked about some shots and key moments. You could tell he was very proud of us.

After a couple of minutes, he asked if he could speak to the other players.

"Okay," I said. "I'm going to hand you to Jamie Korab first."

Before giving the phone to Jamie, I whispered to him, "It's Stephen Harper, the prime minister."

Jamie grabbed the phone from me.

"Hey, Stevie, how are you doing?" he said. "How's the new job treating you?"

Years later, I got to meet Prime Minister Harper again and he brought up the call with Jamie. He thought it was really funny.

The medal ceremony took place on a big concert stage in the medals plaza. There were ten or fifteen thousand people in the crowd, and I thought they were all there to watch us get our medals—until I realized that after we were done there was going to be a concert featuring Ricky Martin. So maybe it wasn't so much about us . . .

I called Mom to describe what was going on and try to let her feel that she was part of everything.

We were backstage with Pete Fenson's U.S. team, who had won the bronze, and of course Markku Uusipaavalniemi's team. We all talked and told stories while waiting for the ceremony to begin.

I remember two things about being on the medal podium.

I remember the playing of "O Canada." We were all standing facing the flag as it was raised and I got filled with emotion. I kept telling myself, *Don't cry, don't cry*. Mark was standing next to me. I remember him saying, "You're okay. You'll get through this."

And then I looked out into the crowd and I saw this one guy wearing a baby blue jacket jumping up and down and waving his arms like crazy. I remember thinking that he didn't really fit in with everyone else. And then I realized who I was looking at.

"Is that Bob?"

Now the whole team was looking at him.

"Yep, I think it's Bob."

"It can't be Bob."

"It has to be Bob."

After the ceremony was done, we were walking out past a fence that separated the audience from the athletes and up comes the guy in his CBC jacket—Bob Cole, who was there to call the men's hockey. It was him jumping up and down and pumping his fists celebrating our gold medals.

Bob was an icon in Newfoundland for all of his accomplishments as a broadcaster. But he had also been a great curler in his time who represented the province in the Brier. And he may well have been our number one supporter, not to mention a great and loyal friend.

Our celebration continued at Canada House, where Canadian Olympians and their families get together at every Olympic Games. Next we went to Vancouver House, which was a log cabin set up in the middle of Turin to promote the upcoming 2010 Winter Games in B.C. It was just a crazy party.

When we got to Vancouver House I was pulled aside to do a bunch of interviews. CBC TV's Peter Mansbridge was there, plus all of the other major Canadian networks. By that point I had knocked back six or seven beers, so I was kind of wondering how I was going to handle being on camera. That's when I noticed a guy who I had seen lingering around me all night, beginning with the stop at Canada House.

I asked Gerry Peckham, the high-performance director for Curling Canada, if he knew who the guy was.

Gerry said, "He's your security detail for the night."

Once we won the gold medal, the IOC had assigned this guy to shadow us and make sure we got back to the village in one piece.

By the time the party at Vancouver House started to die down, all the Olympic transport had shut down for the night. Only the regular city buses were still running.

We stumbled outside and a bus pulled up to the curb. There were half a dozen passengers on board, normal folks going about their late-night business. One of the guards in our security detail got on and started talking to the driver. The next thing we knew, all the passengers got off, and he gestured to our team and our friends, telling us we should get on. The security guard had hijacked the bus to take us back to the village, and these poor people who were just trying to get wherever they were going at two or three in the morning were stranded.

But the remarkable thing was that the folks on the bus were pretty nice about it. We showed them our medals, they took some pictures, and then we hopped on the bus and went back to the village. I don't know how those people ever got home.

I passed out on my bed with my medal on. I slept the whole night with it around my neck.

The closing ceremony was the next day. But by that point, I was just anxious to go home. Even though there was another incredible show to close the Games, I wanted to get back to Newfoundland and see my mom.

The trip home involved a drive from Turin to Milan, a flight to Toronto, and then a flight to St. John's. Needless to say, it was a long journey. Mom was right there at the gate waiting when I got off the plane.

(And I'll mention here that, knock on wood, everything since 2006 has been good with her health. She continues to get regular checkups and there has been no recurrence. It's been twenty healthy years since that first diagnosis, which is amazing.)

The moment I knew that my life had changed was when I got on the escalator at the St. John's airport that takes you down to the baggage claim area. The airport security people had warned me that there were a lot of people there, but nothing they could have said would have prepared me for that scene.

There were people as far as I could see. There were so many that folks were actually being turned away at the entrance to the airport. Coming down that escalator there was a mob scene. You couldn't move. People were coming up to me asking for pictures and autographs. It was a crazy scene. I don't know how long it took us to get out of there.

Our next stop was the St. John's Curling Club, which was as full as I've ever seen it. I think I did eight different interviews that night.

By the time I finally got home it was five or six in the morning.

That pace continued for a long time: the chaos, the lack of sleep, the pressure of always having to be on. No matter where I was, I had to be ready for an interview, ready to pose for a picture, ready for a stranger to come up and want to have a conversation. We had come through the stress of the Olympics and all that goes with it. And then we were dropped into a high-pressure environment back home that we were not accustomed to and that we hadn't trained for. You're just thrust into it, and you're expected to be perfect.

That was a real challenge for me. All of a sudden, it felt like every day I was delivering speeches and doing interviews. It went on like that, day after day, for six or eight months.

The people of Newfoundland kept right on celebrating us and honouring us, which was wonderful. I don't ever want anyone to doubt how much we appreciated that.

If you had told me before the Olympics that we'd win a gold medal and we'd be big stars, I would have thought that was great. But it was also a lot to handle when one minute you're just a normal twenty-five-year-old curler and then overnight you're the most popular person in the province and they're naming highways and streets and schools and parks after you. It's a lot to process.

We had become friends with other Olympians who'd won gold medals and had unbelievable moments, and I remember reaching out to some of them and asking them how they coped with newfound fame. But it was different for them. Nobody had been through what we were going through because no one had been a first-ever Olympic gold medallist from Newfoundland and Labrador. There was no precedent. There was definitely no handbook. We had to figure it out for ourselves.

Krista also had to deal with becoming a public personality. I think she enjoyed the attention more than I did. She liked it when people came up to ask for autographs and pictures. We used to go out to a restaurant for dinner every Friday night and we'd go out to a movie once a week. Those were regular things for us, right up until the Olympics.

Then all of a sudden everything changed, and I became so uncomfortable dealing with all the attention. But Krista wanted to continue our routine. It was a little battle between us. She had been home on her own a lot during the season and the Olympics and naturally she wanted a chance to go out and be social.

Eventually she understood how difficult those situations were for me.

While I might have been a bit short with people who came up to me, Krista was the one who taught me to be patient and to give people their moment. And I've been doing that for the last twenty years.

But I have never really become fully comfortable with it.

In the immediate aftermath of the Olympics, I reacted against all the attention by becoming reclusive. I retreated into myself. I didn't want to go out with friends. I turned into a bit of a loner.

There's also a natural letdown that happens after the Olympics, which is something that not a lot of people talk about. You win the gold medal after years and years working to achieve that. And then the journey is over. The Games are over, and you go home. You have to manage unfamiliar emotions, and it's hard to know how to manage them.

I found that was the case after both Olympics and after every single Brier I've won. When you win, there's a great feeling of satisfaction, and the party afterwards is fun. The next day, you might be dealing with a hangover, but it's still a good feeling, a mixture of elation and relief. And then the day after that, at least for me, it's all over. I start thinking about what comes next.

I think that's where some of the jealousy that I felt for Mark and Jamie and Mike after the Turin Olympics came from. They kept the party going, enjoying the celebration and enjoying the opportunities that came with being Olympic gold medallists in Newfoundland.

Meanwhile, three days after getting home, I was back in the gym and thinking about what we could do as a team to follow up. I was driven by the fear that if I sat back and relaxed and we didn't do it again, people would dismiss me as a fluke, a one-off.

That's where the envy and the animosity crept in. I would look at the other guys enjoying their fame and wonder, "How can you do that?" But part of me also *wanted* to do that. I *wanted* to be like them, but I couldn't be like them.

I reacted by becoming more internal. I dug even deeper into curling, which had always been my sanctuary. I started to practise more and started to work even harder in the gym. That's how I managed my feelings.

That lasted for a little over a year. I didn't hang out with anyone. I didn't go to parties. I just practised and trained, practised and trained.

It was a weird mental process that I was going through after the Olympics and it took me years to understand it better. The truth is, I still don't enjoy my successes anywhere near as much as I should. And I dwell on failures, on losses and missed shots, for way too long.

We kept the gold medal team together for the 2006–7 season, minus Russ, and were very competitive, capping off the year by making the final at the Brier in Hamilton before losing to Glenn Howard.

We were still playing well but we were no longer enjoying ourselves as a team.

All of us had gained a certain level of entitlement, and the dynamic within the team was completely different than it had been heading to the Olympics. The vibe was gone. Life on the road became harder to deal with. We were young guys who'd achieved some incredible success, so egos were a bit out of whack and we were continually weighing the pros and cons of what we were doing on the ice versus what was happening off the ice.

Back home, the gold medal wave just kept rolling. When any of us walked into a restaurant, people would stand and cheer. It couldn't help but change your perception of yourself.

Throughout that season, Jamie wasn't quite working as hard as he should have been. He really loved all the attention but wasn't focusing on his performance. We gave him a number of warnings. We told him he had to work harder and be ready to play. But he didn't take that too seriously. The third time we warned him, it was explicit—if he didn't work harder, we were going to have to make a move. But it didn't seem to sink in with him.

Mark was even more fed up with Jamie's behaviour than I was. Finally, he came to me and told me I had to make a choice: it was either Jamie, or it was him. Mark was so talented and we were so close that it was pretty obvious which way I would go.

I knew that if we dropped Jamie, it would be big news in the curling world, and especially in Newfoundland. I conferred with Toby, and I also met with a public relations company in St. John's about how to handle the announcement. I wanted to make sure we managed things properly and I definitely didn't want to trash Jamie in public.

The advice I got from the PR pros was: "Go right to Jamie, be upfront with him, then put out a press release saying that you're making the change and leave it at that. It will all die down in a day or two."

That was the plan.

We brought Jamie in and told him what we were doing and he was shocked—which shocked us, because we had given him plenty of warnings. He was upset, which wasn't a surprise. You'd expect that from anyone in his situation.

I did a single interview with Robin Short at the *Telegram*. He had followed our team going back to the very beginning of our career, including through the Olympics in Italy, and in those days the newspaper was still the biggest media platform in the province.

I explained our decision without going into detail. I was complimentary about the contributions Jamie made to our team.

Naively, I thought that would be it.

And then Jamie did an interview with Robin that played on the front page of the newspaper. He roasted me pretty good, attacking me personally, attacking my leadership style, attacking how I handled the situation. Overnight, in some people's minds I went from a ten out of ten to a one out of ten because of a single newspaper article.

It was as if the city, and the province, immediately divided into two camps: Either you were on Team Brad or you were on Team

Jamie. If you were supporting Jamie, you hated Brad. At least that's how it felt.

I had made a decision based on what was happening on the ice. It wasn't that we didn't like Jamie anymore. But that's not how people reacted, which was a lesson for me.

Things were particularly bad in the local curling community. I'd go to the same club where I had been going since I was a kid, and people would give me the cold shoulder and say nasty things not just behind my back but right to my face.

People who I thought were friends and supporters weren't friends and supporters anymore. I had phone threats at home—I'd pick up the line and someone on the other end would start calling me names. I even had hate mail. I remember one letter that started off by telling me I should be ashamed of myself and then told me that if I didn't have the patience to deal with Jamie, I was going to be a terrible father. Hayley was not even a year old at the time. That one was really hurtful.

Even though the PR team had assured me it would all be over in a couple of days, things actually went on for weeks. I kept quiet. But Jamie kept doing interviews, one after another, so that anytime it felt like things were dying down, they'd flare up again.

At one point Mark reached out to Robin and told him that he wanted to have his say and get his version of events on the record. Mark wanted everyone to know that it had been a team decision and that he supported it.

But Robin wasn't interested in writing that article. He told Mark that as far as he was concerned, the story was done.

The Jamie situation was particularly hard on Krista. I think of myself as being an emotional person, but she is more emotional than I am, and she was more hurt by the public reaction. It was our decision—mine and Mark's—but Krista unfairly caught some of the flak. One day, when she was working at the hospital, she went in to assess a patient. The person saw her last name on her tag and immediately started telling her about the mistakes I had made—all of that in front of the three other patients in the room.

Krista knew how much I wanted to be fair to Jamie and everybody involved. When the story blew up because of something that was written and completely wrong, she was bothered by that and by how I was being treated.

I know I wasn't the most pleasant person to be around for those months. I was bitter and upset about how it all went down, and Krista had to listen to me day in and day out.

It took a long time for things to get back to normal back home—way longer than it should have. It felt like the controversy was never going to end. We would go out somewhere and run into someone who used to be a friend, and then we would realize that they were now on Team Jamie.

So many relationships were broken during that time, where people I had trusted felt the blowback and jumped ship. It was so disappointing to realize that their loyalty was that frail.

Krista and I changed after that—particularly me. It left scars.

I became very guarded in what I'd share, because I had trusted people and that trust had been broken. I became more shy. My social circle shrank. Even today, I don't allow very many people in. I have a very small group of friends and they're very loyal, and I trust them. I guess that may be why some people think I'm a little bit aloof.

By the time the 2007–8 season began and I headed out on the road, I had kind of weathered the storm at home. But now I had to deal with it all over again within the curling community across the country.

Some of the guys understood—at least from a curling perspective. But Jamie was so well liked and well respected that a lot of people really felt for him. It made it hard for them to look at the situation objectively. I felt like I was back at the centre of the storm and that everybody was against me. I know that wasn't the reality, but it felt like that for a long time.

I learned the hard way that there were a lot of hypocrites in the sport. People said, "Oh my God. What a nasty person Brad is for doing that"—knowing full well that they've made the exact same kind of decision a half-dozen times in their careers.

It happens all the time. There's no competitive team out there that hasn't changed things up at some point. If you want to be one of the best in the world, you have to make tough decisions, and you're going to piss people off. That's just reality.

If you've been a manager of a business or an owner of the business, you've had to let somebody go. It's not easy, but it's necessary.

This is probably the right place to talk about Jamie's *third* go-round with our team—and the third time we let him go. There was the stretch when I was public enemy number one in Harbour Grace, Jamie's hometown, after the first time we cut him. There was the huge blowback after the gold medal. And then in 2009, we wanted to add Ryan Fry to the team, and he wanted to bring Jamie with him. Mark and I went along with it because we knew that group would be formidable.

A lot of people were shocked that we got back together with Jamie, especially after how dark and hateful the situation had been. But from my perspective, there was never any animosity towards him. I didn't love the fact that he went to the media and embellished some stories, and flat out told some lies that made me look bad. I still thought that Jamie was, at heart, a good guy.

I realize now that part of what happened was that he was humiliated by being let go and was trying to save face. He had been so front and centre around the Olympics, and he's such a likeable person and a big personality. Then, all of a sudden, he was out, and maybe worried that people were going to think differently of him, so he protected himself.

For me, bringing him back on the team was a chance to park everything that had happened between us. At that point, it was finally done. It was over.

We had a couple of good years after Jamie came back. We won a Grand Slam together and our team was top five in the world rankings.

But Jamie was dealing with a lot of knee troubles by that point. There weren't any issues with his work ethic this time, but he was having a hard time practising as much as was necessary.

When we decided to make another change at the end of the 2009–10 season and let him go, the parting was much more amicable than it had been the other two times. Jamie understood the decision, and it wasn't really news. The two of us handled it much better. We didn't run to reporters. We didn't air dirty laundry. It was just a normal curling breakup. And we are still friends.

Jamie's oldest daughter, Kendra, and my youngest daughter, Marissa, are roughly the same age. Oftentimes we'll pick up Kendra and bring her down to the curling club, or bring her home from school, and if we can't do it, Jamie will be on carpool duty.

One time Jamie was bringing the girls home, and they were just getting to the age where they were aware that Jamie and I had curled together. Someone told them that I had cut Jamie from the team and, being young and being smart with technology, they decided to Google "Brad Gushue cutting Jamie Korab."

They found all of the articles from the first time we cut him and the second time and the third time. Jamie thought it was hilarious. The girls had a bunch of questions about what happened, and we told them that neither one of us handled the situation as well as we could have.

7

A HOMETOWN BRIER

When it was announced that the 2017 Brier was going to be held in St. John's, I was incredibly excited.

Newfoundland hadn't hosted the tournament since 1972, at the old Memorial Stadium, when it was a much smaller event. By the early 2000s the Brier's popularity had grown enormously and it was being held in huge NHL arenas like the Saddledome in Calgary. We obviously didn't have a venue that size in our province.

But in 2014, when Curling Canada brought the Brier to Kamloops, a city that's a similar size to St. John's, it was a great success. Afterwards I tweeted, "If Kamloops can hold the Brier, why not St. John's?"

When I got back home, Danny Breen, now the mayor of St. John's but then a city councillor, got in touch with me and said, "Let's make this happen."

We put a municipal committee together, came up with a great plan, and sent it off to Curling Canada. The Mile One Centre would be the venue.

I was excited and proud to have been part of that process. But when we got the news in September 2015 that St. John's had been awarded the 2017 Brier, the reality set in that we were going to have to pull it off.

It would be the biggest sporting event in our province's history and there would naturally be tremendous pressure on me and the team to perform. We were the number one team in the world at that point, but I had never won a Brier. Off the ice, I would be the face of the event.

I had some idea of what was coming in terms of the attention and the pressure and the possible distractions, but at least I had months to plan for it. What we couldn't have anticipated was that the next year and a half included both a crazy curling controversy that came to be known as "Broomgate" and me suffering what had to be one of the worst freak injuries in the history of our sport.

During the 2014–15 season our team enjoyed a long stretch of dominance against everybody except for two teams—Mike McEwen and Reid Carruthers. We kept losing against those guys and we couldn't figure out why. They just seemed to have so much more control over the rock than anyone else.

Even when ice conditions were tough, they were making the kind of shots that you make on perfect ice at the Brier or the Olympic trials. When we were struggling just to make contact, they were hitting rocks exactly where they wanted every single time. It was frustrating.

We thought they had our number, that they were good teams that happened to play great against us. They were both in the top five in the world at that point, but we weren't losing to anybody else and yet we were losing to them all the time. We couldn't really answer the question: Why are they beating us?

It never occurred to us that the new Hardline-brand brooms they were using might have had something to do with it. There wasn't much talk about the brooms during that season. Everybody assumed that Mike and Reid were simply playing exceptionally well.

And then at the 2015 Brier in Calgary, there was one rock that Reid threw against us in the first game that should have hit a guard. But when they started to sweep, it actually began to back off from the centre line. We knew that the ice was perfectly level and there was no way the rock should be moving against the curl. That's when the penny dropped. We realized that their brooms might have had something to do with the way they were playing.

That night, we ordered a bunch of the same brooms they were using. When we got back home, we went down to the Bally Haly curling club to test them and realized right away that these things were incredible.

The first thing we noticed was the sound. They made a very loud kind of grinding noise when the head brushed on the ice. And when you examined the head, and you ran your fingernails across it, you could feel the texture and the grittiness of the material. We learned that the manufacturer put a coating on the brush to make it more waterproof, similar to the kind of treatment they use to waterproof a jacket. That coating made the material very hard and very coarse.

There was also a little plastic insert underneath the brush. Taken together, the combination of the materials was harder than the ice surface. When you were sweeping the broom along the ice, you were actually creating little scratches and micro-abrasions that could influence the direction the rock would travel. What's more, those brooms were perfectly legal.

We took some video and sent it to Gerry Peckham, who was the high-performance director for Curling Canada, and told him about all the things we were able to do with these new brooms. We argued that they needed to be banned before things got out of hand.

His message back to us was that there was no plan to ban the brooms.

"My suggestion," he told us, "is that you switch."

At that time, we had a sponsorship deal with a different company, Goldline brooms. After the Players' Championship in 2015, we met with them and worked out an agreement that allowed us to get out of our deal so that we could use any brooms we wanted. Goldline was very understanding about it. We immediately switched to Hardline brooms.

We had been invited to South Korea in the off-season to work with their Olympic teams—we'd coach them for a week and then have four or five days of ice time to ourselves where we could practise.

Our plan was to really focus on the new brooms when we were over there and see what we could get out of them.

When we first got to Korea, we played in a small event and lost 17–1 to a local team because we had no idea what we were doing. We were ruining every single shot that was coming down the ice because we didn't know how to use the brooms properly.

But after we practised a bit we started to figure out how to manage the rocks, and once we did that, we didn't miss a single shot for days.

Mike and Reid had never used brooms to increase the curl of a shot. They always used them to try to keep the rock straight and hold it where it needed to be. We discovered very quickly how to do that, but then we also figured out that if you swept on the high side you could also make the rock curl. We doubled the effect of those brooms by creating that strategy and technique.

We also experimented with using only one sweeper and figured out that it was more effective for directional sweeping than using two. If you had one sweeper on one side and one on the other side, they were actually counteracting each other. By eliminating one side, we could really steer the rock. It allowed the stone to travel farther, and you still had directional control.

The truth is, if we hadn't come up with that strategy, someone else would have soon enough. I'm not claiming we were geniuses. We just caught on sooner and we were smart enough to develop a game plan around it. It ended up changing the sport.

The only question was when to deploy the brooms in competition after we got back to Canada and started the new curling season.

We assumed that people were going to catch on right away to what we were doing. There was a debate within our team: Should we put this in our back pocket and bring it out just before the Brier? Brett was certainly in favour of that option.

My own thinking was that we were the best team in the world and, all things being equal, we were still going to be the best team in the world. So let's go out and make a show of this with our new strategy of employing one sweeper right from the start. We wanted people to know. We didn't want to hide it. Our hope was that once other teams saw us play, the brooms would be banned and we'd get back to regular curling where we felt we already had a big advantage.

But it didn't play out quite that way over the first couple of events. It was remarkable how slowly people caught on. We started out really strong that season, but people mostly made fun of us for only using one sweeper.

I remember when we played a game that was televised on Sportsnet, with Mike Harris and Joan McCusker handling the commentary.

We ticked a guard—which had to be the first guard we had ticked in ten games—and they said, "Well if they had two sweepers they would've got by."

People still hadn't figured out what we were doing, even though they had watched us play multiple games and dominate every single one of them.

To be fair, it had taken the entire previous season of us playing Mike and Reid before we figured things out. But this went on for weeks.

I remember making a shot in a game against Niklas Edin of Sweden where we just got by the guard, and he said to me, "Wow, that rock really straightened out."

"Yeah, it did," I said. But I was thinking, *You should know why it straightened out.* It was because we had one guy sweeping on the inside and didn't have a second sweeper. Niklas is a great curler, but even he couldn't figure it out.

It wasn't until the Stu Sells Cashspiel in Toronto that people started to catch on and the shit really hit the fan.

It was a crazy time. There was a lot of animosity towards Mike and Reid because teams believed they knew what these brooms could do and they'd been hiding it. We were accused of trying to hide what we were doing with the brooms and being manipulative when in fact it was the opposite—we had eight brooms out there, we had one sweeper, we were showing people exactly what was going on. And behind the scenes we had been advocating pretty hard with Curling Canada for the brooms to be banned. We said the same thing to Hardline, even though they were our sponsor.

For a while it turned into the Wild West. There really were no rules. Every company was trying to make their brooms a little stronger, a little lighter. Different materials were being used. One company put some tin foil underneath the fabric of the head that allowed for more heat transfer onto the ice. Another company put heads on both ends of a broom so that they could be changed during shots.

Finally, after we had stirred up enough noise, the World Curling Federation started talking to the players and doing some research. First, the officials got rid of the plastic inserts. That's when we realized that the waterproof coating on the head was just as big an issue.

Then they forced us to put the heads inside out so the waterproofing was on the inside. Later in the year they banned hair brooms (a broom that has horsehair on the head) because they found that the glue that attached the hair to the wood was harder than the ice and it could scratch the ice and alter the path of a stone.

Finally, they limited the number of brooms we could use during a game to one.

(Today when we show up at a big event, they put a little piece of tape on your broom—for a skip, it's green—and that's the broom you have to use throughout the game. You can't change your broom mid-game unless it's damaged, and then you have to get permission from the chief umpire and notify the other team.)

Nowadays, even though the broom's fabric and materials are the same for every team, the techniques that we learned during Broomgate continue to have a huge impact on the sport. It's a different game than the one I played in 2006—more of a sweeping game than it is a shooting and throwing game.

It may be a level playing field when it comes to equipment, but the teams that have really big, strong sweepers are having more success than the pure shooters. They can create a larger window to throw into. It's like playing golf with a hole that's ten times bigger—you're going to make more putts.

Looking back over the past ten years, I don't think those changes have been positive for the sport.

The men's game was better when sweeping wasn't as dominant. Now, especially when you watch some of the high-calibre, high-performance games, it can get kind of boring because teams are making every shot, making doubles and triples and producing a lot of blank ends.

I enjoy the women's game more because they don't have the size and strength that the men have when it comes to sweeping. They'll miss a shot by an inch that the men would make because they can manipulate the rock more with their sweeping. In the women's game you get slightly more variability, a few more misses, and I think that makes it a lot more entertaining.

Even though we had some great results, the whole 2015–16 season felt chaotic. It was a tough one to get through.

And that's even before talking about what happened to me that Halloween.

We were playing in the quarterfinals of a Grand Slam tournament in Truro, Nova Scotia, against Saskatchewan's Steve Laycock. In the fourth end I was standing watching a shot that ran near the boards and I went to move out of the way, something I'd done thousands of times before.

There was a little bit of frost on the sheet that day. Sometimes you get a film on the ice, almost like snow, and it can be slippery if you're not careful.

In trying to avoid the rock I went up on my tippytoes. Then I slipped on some snow and my feet flew out from under me. My hands were on my broom and I couldn't get them out in front of me quickly enough to break my fall.

I landed on the ice right on my forehead.

I remember intense pain and not being able to see. Mark came over and said, "Let me have a look at it." When I dropped my hands, I could tell he was completely grossed out. It turned out that my brow was split open and the skin had come down over my eye. There was a lot of blood on the ice. It was pretty gruesome.

The guys got me off the ice and took me to the hospital, which fortunately was right across the street from the arena. I asked the doctor to stitch me up fast so I could get back to the game. I went through a quick concussion protocol, and as far as anyone could tell I didn't have any issues. The doctor cleaned me up, put some stitches in, put a bandage on my forehead, and then I booted it back across the street.

By then it was the eighth end and the game was tied.

I walked into the rink and as soon as I saw the TV lights my head started to throb. But the crowd was cheering and I felt I couldn't just turn around and walk back out.

I went out and threw my rocks. The first shot I made. The second one I missed by an absolute mile.

In hindsight, it was a stupid decision to go back out there. I should never have been allowed on the ice.

The doctor gave me permission to fly, and that night I headed home to St. John's. The next day, I woke up with an intense headache and nausea—classic concussion symptoms. I went to see my own doctor, who was disgusted by the stitching job on my eye and amazed that anyone had let me fly home. (I took responsibility for the messy stitches because I was putting pressure on the doctor to get it done fast so I could get back into the game.)

I spent the next ten days in a darkened room waiting for the concussion symptoms to clear. The only reason I got out was to play another event—and the truth is, I should have waited longer. But I didn't want to miss out and I didn't want to let down my teammates.

It was another big mistake.

I wound up dealing with concussion symptoms for the rest of that curling season, and it took me forever to get rid of the black eye.

There was one funny part of the story. On Halloween in Newfoundland, I'd heard that some of the kids went out dressed as Brad Gushue—they painted on black eyes and walked around carrying brooms.

When I came back from my fall, even though I wasn't feeling right, we were still pretty successful. We won a couple of Slams but then ended up losing in the Brier final to Kevin Koe in Ottawa.

There were still some shenanigans going on with brooms and some of the new rules hadn't kicked in yet.

Kevin's team had developed a strategy where they put aside a broom that they didn't use in practice—sometimes they didn't even use it early in the game—because as soon as you used a broom and gave it a couple of strokes, you started to wear down that waterproofing material. With each stroke, its effect was reduced. When they brought it into play fresh, they could use it to carve a rock and get it to curl really hard. During the first two or three ends of every single game in that Brier, Team Koe was pretty dominant. You had to get through those couple of ends until their broom wasn't as sharp and the playing field levelled again.

When we played them in the Brier final, there were some situations in the first few ends when we were in a really good position to score multiple points. But then Koe's team would play a shot where they got the outside guy to sweep hard with the broom that hadn't been used and curled the rock into a position where it was really difficult to remove.

That surprised us. We went into the Brier operating under the assumption that everybody was employing the sweeping style that had been the norm for the past twenty years. But Koe's team had found an edge. They found a way to maximize the brooms they had and they'd obviously practised it. And we got burned by it. We could have done the same thing, but we believed it would be too much of a risk to change our strategy all of a sudden.

In the first end, we had a rock in the top twelve. Kevin played a draw, and they used that sharp broom to bury their rock where I couldn't get at it with my final shot. I had to play a double raise, which I ended up missing and we fell behind immediately. They stole another point in the second end and went on to win the game pretty easily. The final score was 9–5.

While I was recovering from the concussion, I had started to feel a pinch in my hip and groin area when I was sliding. Starting a game, during my first five or six slides I would feel a very sharp pain. But as I slid more and more, it would eventually loosen up, and by the time I got to mid-game I wasn't feeling it too much at all.

That continued throughout the year, from shortly after my fall until the end of the season. I thought I'd get some rest over the summer, get some treatment, and be ready for the start of the new season in September.

But then I got a call from the World Curling Federation telling me that they were going to hold a sweeping summit in May in Gatineau, Quebec. They wanted Mark and me to be part of the testing and to provide some input on how sweeping might evolve in the game. They didn't want to have another season like the one we had just experienced. The National Research Council would help with the testing.

We were among a group of a dozen curlers from around the world who were invited. Because I was playing at such a high level and I could throw so consistently, they wanted me to throw most of the rocks as a way of eliminating as many variables as possible.

When I went to slide for the first time, the stabbing and pinching in my hip and groin became way more intense—to the point where I fell down because the pain was so bad.

I thought that if I took another five or six slides, I could get the hip warmed up the way I had during the season. Then I took another slide and I fell down again. I took another one and I fell down again.

I realized that I was not okay.

Fortunately, Curling Canada was able to get me in for an MRI right away. It showed that I had an impingement but that the injury was probably muscular rather than any structural damage in the hip joint.

I stayed for the summit and provided my input, but I didn't throw any more.

When I got home, I sought out some sports medicine people to help me. For a while, I was making a little headway. But as we started to get closer to the start of the season, I realized my hip wasn't getting better—in fact it was probably getting worse. I was frustrated and anxious, knowing that I was still far away from being able to throw.

I made another attempt when we got back on the ice in September. This time, the pain was even worse than I had experienced at the summit. I hadn't been able to throw normally since May, and it didn't look like I was going to be able to do it anytime soon.

It was suggested that I go and see Dr. Andrew Furey, who was a world-class orthopedic trauma surgeon who would go on to become the premier of Newfoundland and Labrador. He did some tests, agreed that the injury was mostly muscular, and referred me to a doctor in Toronto named Danny Whelan.

I went up and got all kinds of testing done—in one day I had an MRI, a CT scan, and X-rays.

Danny helped me connect to a couple of other specialists, and then I flew home, where Andrew put me in touch with a physiotherapist named Liv Martyn. Once she started working with me I made some progress. Liv introduced me to Kate Boone, a massage therapist, who is still working with me ten years later.

All that fall, I'd see Kate and Liv twice a week.

At the end of November, I arranged to go down to the curling club early one morning, at a time when I knew nobody would be around. It was just me and Krista and Harold, the ice maker and manager at the club. I needed to see if I could slide.

The first time I tried, I felt that stabbing pain again. I got so mad that I banged my broom and screamed "For fuck's sake!" as loud as I could.

Krista didn't love that reaction.

I took another slide and it was slightly better. And another one—it was a little better again. Maybe I was finally on the mend.

Kate, Liv, and I put in another four weeks together, and then I came back to play the last Slam before Christmas. I was still in a significant amount of pain. I couldn't throw any more than ten and a half seconds, which is pretty light, but I got through it and we still ended up making it to the semifinals.

So that was interesting—our team was so good that even if I wasn't at full strength, we could get to the semi of a Slam.

For the next month, I continued with the rehab. Then we played another Slam in January and I was up to a nine-second hit, which is our normal weight. We ended up winning that one.

In order to qualify for the Brier, we had to win the Newfoundland provincials.

That turned out to be a real battle, not so much because of the competition but because the ice conditions were bad for my hip. As the ice got worn down, there wasn't enough air circulation between the pebbles and the slider on my shoe, which made it feel like I was attached by a suction cup during my delivery. That really aggravated my sore hip.

But we won, leaving us five weeks until St. John's.

Something else, profoundly important, was happening during 2017.

Krista's father, Harvey, had been waiting for over a year for a lung transplant. Over that year his health had started to deteriorate to the point where he and Krista's mom, Marie, moved to Toronto to be close to the transplant centre so that Harvey could go into surgery as soon as a donor organ became available.

It was all about waiting for the call. Each week that went by, Harvey's lungs were getting worse and worse, and it was getting harder and harder for him to breathe.

Finally, in February, a week before the Brier, they found out that there was a single lung that was a good match. Harvey was booked for surgery, and of course Krista flew to Toronto to be with him. I can only imagine the emotions she was going through with her father in a life-and-death situation while at the same time dealing with me and with everything going on back home.

The transplant went really well. Harvey and Marie were able to watch the Brier from his hospital room in Toronto. I think it was a happy distraction for them during the early part of his recovery.

8

THE 2017 BRIER

I have never worked so hard at anything—seeing Liv, seeing Kate, doing the exercises, doing everything I could to make sure I was as physically ready to play in what would be one of the biggest events of my life.

Our team knew that the challenge at the Brier was going to extend beyond what we did on the ice. These were unique circumstances.

Newfoundland is a different kind of place. We are a small province, at least in terms of population, that has faced a lot of challenges. We certainly don't have the number of athletes or otherwise famous people that a lot of other provinces have. And as I've mentioned, we passionately support our own. If one of our guys makes the NHL, it's a big deal. All Newfoundlanders share in their success and they become some of the biggest celebrities in our community.

If the Brier were held in Brandon or Winnipeg, it would be a different sort of event. There are lots of hockey players from Manitoba who are famous. They have their own CFL and NHL teams, and they have also produced a lot of well-known musicians and actors.

But in Newfoundland, when someone makes it to the national stage, whether it's in the NHL or curling or as an actor or musician or writer, no one takes it for granted and everyone gets behind them in a really intense way.

The 2017 Brier was the biggest sporting event that our province had ever hosted. And since the 2006 Olympics, we were some of the biggest celebrities Newfoundland had ever produced—at least in the eyes of Newfoundlanders. That meant we were going to have to deal with something far different from what an Alberta rink would face playing a Brier in Alberta, or an Ontario rink in Ontario. The level of interest in us was going to be off the charts.

When the Brier comes to your hometown and you are literally the focus of the event, people naturally want a piece of you. It can take a toll on you physically, mentally, and emotionally.

Our team wanted to find a way to minimize that as much as possible. I knew that what I was going to go through that week was far different than what Kevin Koe was going to go through, or Brad Jacobs or Mike McEwen were going to go through.

It may sound strange, given that in sports we talk all the time about a home-field advantage, but we actually needed a way to make the playing field a little bit more level.

Way back in June 2016 we decided to develop a plan to help us deal with all the distractions that we knew were coming. We put it on paper—eight or nine pages by the time we finished it—and worked on it with our sports psychologist, Kyle Paquette, and our coach, Jules Owchar.

Our plan included everything from how we were going to walk to the arena in order to avoid crowds as best we could, to where we were going to eat our meals, to how we were going to interact with family and friends, to what would happen if we were late for a game or if a game was late in starting.

We knew we were going to have issues with people wanting a bunch of our time. Kyle talked to us about how that could be a trap. When you're with people and you're on a winning streak, or you're coming off a tough loss, their emotions and energy can transfer onto you and end up having a detrimental effect on your mindset. You lose and they express their sympathies, you win and you get all of their excitement. Kyle said it was important to try to avoid those ups and downs and stay on an even keel.

But how could we avoid all these distractions in a fishbowl like St. John's, where we would be going out to eat, where we would be walking to the rink, in plain sight? How would we manage family and friends, who we still wanted to be with but who would also be feeling those same emotions?

You name it, we tried to prepare for it. We were going to do our best to control what we could control. By planning—and maybe overplanning—we thought we could ease the nerves we knew we were going to feel during the competition.

We spent a day in a private room at the Merchant Tavern in St. John's working through how we thought the week would play out. The next day we moved to Bally Haly and spent another day working on our plan in one of their boardrooms. We drew on our experiences playing in other Briers and at the Olympic trials and talked about what we could do better preparing for the kind of moments that might create anxiety. Finally, this is what we came up with:

Team Gushue 2017 Brier Plan
Bally Haly Country Club, June 10, 2016

Hotel/accommodations

- Brad to inquire about five rooms or suite at the Delta Hotel
- Brad to contact Danny Lamoureux of Curling Canada to confirm accommodations

Arena

- Brad and Mark to meet with Brier committee
  - ✓ Confirm driver accreditation
  - ✓ Confirm back door entrance/exit to Mile One Centre
  - ✓ Confirm access to IceCaps dressing room
  - ✓ Confirm access for the team's massage therapists

Driver

- Find personal driver for the team who is professional, dependable, and quiet

Meals/restaurants

- Confirm breakfasts in hotel
- Confirm access to the Merchant Tavern for team meals
- Mark to contact Jorie Janzen (create nutrition guidelines)
- Mark to send guidelines to chef Jeremy Charles at the Merchant Tavern
- Mark to conceptualize plan with Jeremy Charles

Coach

- Brad to contact Jules Owchar about coaching duties
- Preparation events:
  - ✓ The Masters (Okotoks, AB)
  - ✓ Canada Cup (Brandon, MB)
  - ✓ Canadian Open (North Battleford, SK)

Support team

- Confirm a handler for Up Close and Personal and Autograph sessions organized by Curling Canada
- Revisit all of the points once we receive the schedule
- Kyle to:
  - ✓ Finalize nine-day taper meal plan with Mark's help
  - ✓ Develop relationship with Jules, connect with him throughout Brier
  - ✓ Preparation camp in Ottawa
  - ✓ Team chats: midweek, prior to playoffs, finals
  - ✓ Individual chats: flexible
- Brad to organize physiotherapy

Friends and family
- Confirm family box for games (Brad to contact Danny Lamoureux)
- Obtain burner phones (for Brad and Mark)
- Look into prepaid SIM cards
- Discuss needs and expectations of the tournament with everyone

Media/social media
- Brad to contact Plum Creative Works to handle PR
- Find social media coordinator
- Schedule a media day (Friday, February 24)
- Forward all media requests to coordinator

Fatigue management
- Follow nine-day taper plan
- No access to media/social media
- No watching curling
- Scheduled naps
- Daily extended meditation sessions

Brier obligations
- Brad to contact Danny Lamoureux regarding:
  ✓ Up Close and Personal
  ✓ Autograph session

We decided that we would move out of our homes during the Brier and stay downtown at the Delta Hotel, which was a short walk from the arena. The event organizers offered us the use of the dressing room that belonged to the local AHL IceCaps hockey team as our own private space.

Normally when we compete, I like to arrive at the venue an hour before the game. But if I did that in St. John's, I'd be arriving at the same time as the bulk of the crowd. So instead, I went to the rink over two hours early, when most of the fans were still inside the building watching one of the earlier games or hanging out at the Brier Patch.

If I ran into a few people along the way, I stopped to sign autographs or pose for a picture. But at least it wasn't a mob scene.

We would be playing mostly night games, so I could hang out in the dressing room and get my treatment done on my hip.

It was also suggested that whoever we added as our fifth for the Brier should be someone who knew the game well enough that he could help support us doing all the little things that needed to be done but that I didn't necessarily want to do—and also a guy who could act as a sort of bodyguard/assistant to help get me to the rink and avoid the crowds.

Geoff suggested a buddy of his, Tom Sallows. They grew up together around Grande Prairie, Alberta, and had played on the same team for a couple of years.

Tom turned out to be great. At times when I was feeling overwhelmed, just having someone else to talk to was a big asset. He would have some food waiting for me when I got to the rink early and then the other guys would stroll over closer to our starting time.

For the rest of our meals, chef Jeremy Charles, who was then at the Merchant Tavern, agreed to take care of us and serve us in a private space in the restaurant where no one else could see us—it was actually the old vault in what had been a bank before the building became a restaurant. Tom would call ahead to give Jeremy fifteen minutes' notice and he would lay out a family-style meal of five or six dishes. It was incredible, healthy food, and we would be in and out in a flash.

After the games, I'd get treatment, we'd go into the hot tub, and it would be an hour and a half after the last shot was played before I'd head back to the hotel. By that time the building would have cleared out.

So that was the plan. And by and large, it worked.

But the reality of that Brier was way more than any of us could have anticipated.

When we walked into the Mile One Arena for our first pre-event practice, hundreds of people were there to watch us. That never happened at any event, anywhere.

Next came the Hot Shots, a skills competition that they used to hold before the Brier where the winner gets a car. A couple of thousand fans showed up for that.

I didn't feel good at all that day. My leg was shaking because it was so tight. All I could think was, *Stay on your feet. Don't fall down in front of this crowd.* I knew that every single eye in the building was on me. In the end I still managed to perform pretty well and finished third.

The process of making and implementing our plan at least made us feel like we were prepared for whatever might be thrown at us. And it felt that way right up until we got to the first game and the reality hit me. I was shaky, even if it didn't look like it on TV.

We were playing Alberta's Brendan Bottcher. Fortunately for us, that was his first time at a Brier, so his team was just as nervous as we were—and that's saying something, because we were very, very nervous.

Our team really struggled in that game, but I actually curled 100 percent—though in retrospect I don't know how I did it, because I couldn't feel my body. We won 8–6.

The second game was against Mike McEwen's team from Manitoba and we wound up losing pretty badly. I was limping when I came off the ice.

When Liv and Kate saw the way I was walking, they knew that it was going to take a lot of work just to keep me on the ice. They worked on my hip for two or three hours that night and then told me they would be waiting for me at the arena before every game to get me ready and would be there afterwards for as long as I needed them to help me recover.

From that point on, I had to be treated before and after every game just to be able to go out and play. Without Liv and Kate there is zero chance we would have won that Brier. (And in the end, it wasn't just me. Later in the week, Geoff blew out his shoulder and needed treatment as well.) Those two were the unsung heroes of our team.

Our record was 3–1 when we went in against Jamie Koe's rink from the Northwest Territories.

Now, understand that I love our coach, Jules Owchar. He's great.

But before that game, for reasons known only to him, he decided to come up and tell me: "No team has ever lost to the Northwest Territories and then gone on to win the Brier."

Jules, why would you say that right now?

We were down 3–1 early and couldn't come back, finally losing 8–4. Our record was 3–2, which wasn't so bad, but we were just not the same team. We weren't communicating well. We were playing poorly. We were at each other. Our body language wasn't good. You could tell we were stressed and feeling the pressure of the tournament.

I had to do a media scrum immediately after the game. When that was finished, the four of us plus all of our support staff—massage, physio, sports psychologist, coach—got together in our dressing room.

I could sense that something wasn't right.

"Guys, what's going on?" I said. "We're not ourselves."

Nobody said a thing until finally, Mark piped up.

"I'm not comfortable," he said. "I'm feeling the pressure. It's a lot. We've got all our friends and family here. We're playing poorly. We're not enjoying it." He said he was having trouble sleeping and eating.

And then Brett spoke up, and said he felt the same way. Geoff and I shared the same feelings. We went around the room. Everybody was in the same place.

You know the expression "A burden shared is half a burden"? Talking about it took a weight off our shoulders.

If you go back and watch those first five games, we were like machines. We were robots out there. No emotion. We seemed afraid to really express ourselves.

Part of what we had talked about leading up to the Brier was getting the crowd behind us, getting them excited. Why should we be afraid to pump our fists if we made a good shot?

We decided that in the next game we were going to go out and show some emotion. If someone missed a shot, they would bang their broom and let the crowd know that they were pissed off—without allowing it to affect the next shot. And if we did something great, we would celebrate it.

We came out full of piss and vinegar in the next game, against Brad Jacobs, ready to go.

Before a game starts, you have a draw to the button to decide who starts with the hammer. This is actually very important—if you start the game with the hammer, you win 60 percent of the time. Against a team as good as Brad's, the odds might be even higher. I needed to win that draw.

They measure the shots from the pinhole, but if you cover the pin they triangulate to see how perfect your draw is.

Brad went first and made his draw. The rock stopped 1.8 centimetres from perfect.

When we saw that, all that piss and vinegar immediately disappeared. I could see my teammates' shoulders drop. This was not what we needed.

The odds of getting inside 1.8 centimetres are maybe one in one hundred. I got in the hack for my shot and I thought I'd try to get it as close as I could and then let the guys sweep it home.

Coming down to the hog line, the line looked good. It was just a matter of getting the weight right.

The rock stopped and it was close. I looked over the top and it seemed flawless.

We were waiting for the triangulation to happen and the number to come up on the screen. And then it was there: 1.2 centimetres.

Holy shit.

We freaking celebrated. We were pumped. The game started and we were immediately into it.

Brad's team made a mistake in the first end, leaving us an open hit for two points—as simple a shot as you could ever imagine. I threw, made the shot, and then jumped up and pumped my fist as though I had just made a raise double takeout.

We were embracing the passion of the crowd and it was paying off. I've got to imagine that for the other teams playing against us, it must have been challenging, knowing that there were 6,500 people in that building who didn't want them to win.

The second end was the exact opposite. It was wide open until we made a mistake, leaving Jacobs an open draw for two. His guys were famous back in those days for being pretty intense. As the rock came into the house they were shouting, "Let's go—let's fucking go!"

They got their two and now the game was really on.

We went back and forth until the eighth end, when we were up by a point with the hammer, but Brad made a really nice shot with his final rock. I was left having to chase it with a back-line tap, but I was going to have to squeak by one of our stones to get to it.

I threw the shot. It had lots of room to get by the guard. And then all of a sudden it started to curl. It started to curl a lot.

The sweepers got on it. I was screaming as hard as I could. Mark was screaming. The crowd was screaming. We squeaked by our rock in the top of the eighth and scored two.

I remember at that point turning around and giving a fist pump and then lifting my hands to get the crowd going. The roar was so frigging intense. It was the loudest thing I'd ever experienced in my life. It gave me chills like you wouldn't believe.

We held them to one in the ninth to win it 7–5.

All of a sudden, we were a different team and got on a run for the rest of the week.

In the round robin we played a really good game against Kevin Koe. I ended up having to draw the button in an extra end for the win, and I made it.

When we got to the final, we wound up playing Kevin again. I remember being very nervous but also very comfortable—at peace with the situation.

We were pretty oblivious inside our self-imposed bubble, but I learned afterwards that the atmosphere in the province was a lot like it had been during the 2006 Olympics. They didn't have to close the schools because the final was on the weekend. But local businesses had nobody in their stores when the game was on. It seemed like everybody in the province was either home watching us on TV or at the arena.

The sound in that building was absolutely unbelievable. I talked to Vic Rauter, who was doing the TSN broadcast, and he said that it was the loudest building he'd ever been in. The atmosphere was just so electric.

We started out great. Our first five ends were just about as perfect as you could get. In the sixth end, we were up 5–1 when we made a bit of a mistake and Kevin made a great shot to score three and pull within one.

The last few ends became more of a struggle after that. You could tell that their team found some energy and we were just holding on.

In the ninth end, we were up by one without the hammer. Kevin was going really hard to try to score two points and we were trying to force him to one. Marc Kennedy, his third, made a good shot, and I had to throw my next rock well to pick it up.

With his first stone, Kevin came tighter to the guard and got it top twelve. I could see maybe an inch and a half of it. The option was to play a draw on the other side, which we hadn't played in a long time, or to try to pick that rock out. If we picked it out, worst case was we'd be tied with the hammer coming home. We opted for the pick.

When I let the rock go, it was one of those shots that just clicks. It fell right into the slot. I knew it was perfect. In that moment, with all that pressure, I remember calling, "Clean!" I could just feel it.

As the rock came down the sheet and was just shy of the hog line, I was thinking, *I need to go to the bathroom before the tenth end.* That's how confident I was that I had made it.

I fist-pumped to the crowd, and then I went straight to the bathroom.

While I was in there, I was hoping to hear a big cheer, because that would mean Kevin had missed his last shot and the game was over.

Instead, I heard a cheer building, followed by a little groan at the end. They swept Kevin's shot hard and just got it home to tie the game.

I wish I had seen that shot, because those guys had to work their tails off to get that rock all the way down the side of the ice where we hadn't played a lot of shots.

We played really well in the tenth. I was left with an in-turn draw to the eight-foot on the same side where Kevin had just played his draw—the shot that I didn't see—if I wanted to win the Brier.

The ice was starting to run slow. I remember Brett saying to me, "It's six feet heavier here," which is a lot. That was a big difference from what I'd been throwing all week. The ice had been so consistent that I could throw the same weight and it would stop on the tee line every time. It was automatic.

But now, with the chance to make a simple shot and fulfill a childhood dream, Brett was telling me that it was six feet heavier. That's not what you want to hear in that situation.

I trusted Brett fully. I believed him when he said it was six feet heavier. But my adrenaline was pumping, and I also trusted our sweepers. If I gave them an extra two feet or even four feet, they could work the rest of it.

I gave the shot a little extra than what I had been throwing.

When I let it go, Brett said, "It looks good."

But there was one other complication.

Geoff's injured shoulder meant that he was having real trouble sweeping. According to the rules, we couldn't change the lineup at that point in the match. Mark was still going to have to hold the broom. But as soon as I let go of the shot, he could run out and help.

When he got there and joined Brett sweeping, Mark shouted, "It doesn't look heavy." About a third of the way down the sheet, they really started to go. Geoff was standing off to the side and the two of us were screaming, while Mark and Brett were going all out.

When the rock crossed the hog line, I didn't think it was going to get there. I had a moment where I was thinking, *Oh my God, I just missed another draw of the eight-foot to win a Canadian championship.* That's what was going through my head.

But the guys never quit. The rock got closer to the rings and I realized that it was going to make it to the four-foot. That's when I knew that we were going to win.

Ultimately the rock stopped just six inches past where it needed to be.

I threw my hands up in the air and let go of the broom—it flew twenty feet over my head. It was as much a release of tension and stress as it was excitement. The pressure on all of us had been so intense. And suddenly, it was gone.

What happened next was pretty magical.

Everyone in the crowd stayed in their seats for the whole closing ceremony. Not a single person left the building.

Krista and I hugged, and she said to me: "It's over."

She wasn't just talking about the Brier, but about her father, about the months of stress and pressure, about my injury and the doubt about whether I was even going to be able to curl that season, about the spotlight we were all under at home in St. John's. It was a lot, especially for her and our family.

After that we had pictures taken, then went back to the dressing room to do our drug testing. We filled out the necessary forms to register for the world championships, had a few celebratory beers, and then the organizers came over and asked if we wanted to head for the Brier Patch.

By now, it was hours after the final shot.

When we went across the street to the convention centre, home of the Brier Patch, I was shocked by how many people were there. There were two thousand people inside and a thousand more outside trying to get in. And this was a Sunday night. In theory, everyone had to go to work the next day.

It was probably 1:30 a.m. by the time we made our way up on the stage. I was carrying the original 1927 Brier tankard.

The roar from the crowd was incredible.

I asked Mark if he thought we should pass the trophy around. He didn't say anything, but his eyes got really big. I thought it was a great idea.

I handed the tankard to the crowd and away it went.

The Curling Canada officials onstage, however, weren't so thrilled. I will never forget the look of shock and anger on their faces. I had just sent their historic trophy into what looked like a mosh pit.

There was a second there when I worried that maybe this wouldn't end well. But I should have had more faith in our fans. The trophy circled around, was touched by thousands of people, and then was returned unharmed back to the stage.

(When we won the Brier the next time, Curling Canada had the original trophy on the podium, but as soon as the camera lights went off, they took it away and a replica was waiting for us in the dressing room. I guess they learned their lesson in 2017.)

When the Brier Patch finally shut down in the wee hours, our party moved over to the Delta Hotel, where we had been staying. We kept it going there until eight in the morning.

When I finally passed out for a few hours of sleep, the tankard was with me in my hotel bed.

After all was said and done, I remember thinking, *Man, I'm not sure I want to do that again.* I was so emotionally spent and so tired. (Little did I know that there would be another hometown Brier in 2026, and that it would be my career swan song.)

A few weeks later the world championship was held in Edmonton. We were representing our country as Team Canada, playing in front of 12,000 people, but that felt like nothing compared to what it was like playing in front of those 6,500 people in St. John's. On the ice, it was magical. I felt this crazy sense of relief in my body. There was no pressure at all. It was the best performance our team has ever had, and I'd argue that any team in the history of curling would have had a hard time beating us that week. We were so good. All four of us played so well. And I think that personally, a big part of that came from the fact that I was relieved that all my curling goals had now been achieved. I had checked the last box on that list in my bedroom. The guys saw how relaxed I was and it freed them up to play their absolute best.

I remember one particular moment when I was leaving the ice headed for the dressing room, and I was thinking, *This is fun, I feel so good.* I walked by some volunteers and I engaged with them. I wasn't in that hyper-focused tunnel where I usually found myself at big events, stressed to the max. That one time, it was just carefree.

We ran the table, finishing 13–0. Not once did any of those games even go to last rock. The closest was the final against Niklas Edin (who we had already beaten twice along the way), but we won that game pretty easily too. That victory made me the first skip in the history of the sport to win a world juniors, a world title, and an Olympic gold medal.

I've never been able to replicate the way I felt in Edmonton. It was the most fun I have ever had curling, tension-free, as though we were playing with house money. They talk about being "in the zone," that magical place, in the world of sports psychology. For one week I found it. And I've worked for the last eight years wondering how to get back there.

I realize now that part of what was happening then was that I didn't have time to recalculate. The monkey was off my back in terms of winning that first Brier, and I hadn't had time to sit down and figure out what my next goals were. I was in this wonderful kind of middle world where it felt like I had achieved everything and wasn't pushing for anything more.

After that world championship, that changed pretty quickly. A new year was coming. I had to figure out what my goals were now.

I never went as far as writing them down on a sheet of bristol board. But it was head down, back to business, focusing on the coming season.

That's the way it has stayed ever since.

At the end of our 2016–17 season, Tom Sallows—our fifth and my "bodyguard" at the Brier—invited us to northern Alberta, where he worked as an outfitter, for a few days of camping and kayaking and fishing.

People who know me will tell you that I'm a bit of a princess. I love the outdoors but I'm not a camper—camping for me is staying at a Holiday Inn. I like my creature comforts. But I knew Tom would take care of us, and he had all the gear, so I agreed to go along with Geoff and Brett.

Tom had everything planned. He had gone on a hunting trip the week before and got an elk and some fish, so we were going to eat very, very well throughout the week.

We drove for three hours north of Grande Prairie way out into the bush—really the middle of nowhere. Our plan was that on the second day we were going to do a kayaking trip that Tom said he had done when he was a teenager. "I know the river pretty well," he said. "There's one spot in there where there's a waterfall that's fairly big, but we'll be fine."

Tom had inflatable kayaks that took us half a day to blow up. When we were finally ready, I figured we were in for a leisurely trip downriver.

"Do you have any lifejackets?" I asked Tom.

"No. You don't need to worry about that," he said. "If you fall into the river—which isn't going to happen—just stand up. There's going to be nothing deeper than your waist or your stomach."

"Do you have any helmets?" I asked him.

"No," he said. "There's nothing dramatic on this river."

I mentioned the waterfall.

"When you get to that," Tom said, "just make sure that you lean back as you're going down."

It was a cold day, kind of drizzly, maybe five or six degrees when we started on our trek. Ten minutes in, I could hear a faint roar off in the distance.

"That's the waterfall coming up," Tom said.

It was maybe a four-foot waterfall—fairly significant for an inflatable kayak, but nothing too serious, and we got through without any problem.

A little farther down the river we came to another waterfall that was perhaps five feet high.

"Maybe this is the one that I remember being the big one," Tom said. We got through it with no issues.

I'm actually a pretty good kayaker. I've done it a lot over the course of my life. Brett and Geoff weren't quite as experienced, so they fell back a little and I got out ahead of the group.

I came around a corner and I could hear a rumble in the distance. By then I was in a kind of small canyon with high banks on both sides. I started to paddle backwards and grabbed on to a tree on shore because I didn't know what was ahead—other than that from its sound it was clearly another waterfall.

Tom pulled up beside me.

"I think this may be the big one," I said.

He got out and walked downriver to have a look.

Then he walked back to me. "Holy shit," he said. "This one is huge."

That's not necessarily what you want to hear from your guide.

Brett had caught up with us. Because he wasn't a great kayaker the current kind of caught him and pushed him downstream towards the waterfall. At this point I had no idea how big it actually was—it could have been two hundred feet high for all I knew.

Tom and I were both screaming at him.

"Square up! Square up!"

"Lie back! Lie back!"

If you go down a waterfall sideways instead of square, you'll topple end over end.

Brett disappeared over the falls. And the thought going through my head was, *Oh my God, he's dead.*

A few moments later, we heard Brett shouting.

"Holy shit! I'm alive. I made it!"

Geoff had joined us by that point and had managed to grab hold of a tree. But we knew there was no real way out of this. We couldn't climb out of the canyon. We had to keep going.

Geoff went first. Then I told Tom that I'd be okay going last, and he pushed off and headed downriver. The last thing he said to me was, "Just make sure you go right down the middle of this waterfall."

As I said, I'm a pretty good kayaker. I hit the falls right in the middle. I was perfectly squared up. And then I hit a rock that was also right in the middle of the falls and I went over into the water.

That was a bit of a shock.

I immediately thought about what Tom had told me: "You just have to stand up."

I went to stand up and then started sinking and sinking fast. The river at that point had to be ten or twelve feet deep and my rainsuit started filling up with water.

I managed to get myself up to the surface and found a rock that I could hold on to. Eventually I found a way out of that predicament with the help of the other guys. We've got some great pictures and videos of me stranded in the middle of the falls.

(When I got home and told Krista what had happened, she was so mad at me.)

I admit that the amount of risk we took on that trip was ridiculous. But looking back, it was such a great team-building moment for us.

The next day we went fishing—and that was pretty tame.

9

DECEMBER 10, 2025

Heading into the Olympic trials in Halifax I was feeling pretty confident about where I was at. I had some really good practices and loved how I was throwing the rock. I was making a ton of shots.

Physically, I was dealing with a little pain and discomfort. But Kate, our massage therapist, was going to be there, and generally when she's with us things don't get worse, so I wasn't too worried.

The one concern I had was that Mark had been struggling during our preparation for the trials. There was some tension around our team trying to get him to his normal level. We need Mark to be Mark to win. If he wasn't at his best, it was going to be an uphill battle for all of us.

But one thing about Mark—he always shows up for the big events. In our first game against Rylan Kleiter of Saskatchewan, he came out and looked like his old self. All the struggles that he had during our training camp disappeared and he started throwing the rock like he normally does. I could tell that his attitude and his demeanour were where we needed them to be, and that's a big reason why we got off to a great start that week.

A lot of people who saw us play were talking about the old Gushue magic being back, and to be honest, that's exactly how it felt.

After that solid first game against Kleiter we had a good feel for the ice at the Scotiabank Centre. We played Kevin Koe next, and it turned out to be one of the most enjoyable, fun games I've played in my career.

Kevin was vintage Kevin that day. He was making triples, making runbacks. He played at an exceptionally high level, but so did our team. Mark played great, Brendan was great, and Geoff was great.

We ended up winning to run our record to 2–0 in the qualifying round. Then we went out against John Epping of Ontario and played another great game to make it 3–0. Our confidence was really starting to build.

Then, in our fourth game, things went off the rails.

We were playing Manitoba's Matt Dunstone, and both teams were undefeated. It looked like that could be the game for first place, because Brad Jacobs already had a loss. If we finished first in the round robin, we'd get a bye to the best-two-out-of-three final.

The Dunstone game was when we started to see some of the same cracks that had shown up during our training camp. Mark missed a few shots, Brendan missed a few shots, and I was left playing some shots that had a pretty high degree of difficulty. If I missed, we would be out of the game.

It all came down to an extra end, with Matt having the hammer. I made a great last shot on my last one, forcing Matt to throw it really hard and attempt a shot that not a ton of people can make.

He made it and we lost that game—and in the end, that's the shot that cost us the tiebreaker to get into the playoff.

After that loss we assumed it was going to be almost impossible to get past Matt and finish in first place. He had been playing so well all year and we just couldn't see him losing twice. (Little did we know he'd go on to lose three times in the run of the tournament.)

Our next game was against Manitoba's Jordon McDonald, one of the young teams at the trials. Someone pointed out to me that no one on Jordon's rink was born when I played my first Brier. That sure made me feel old. Watching Jordon and his teammates on the ice reminded me of the way we must have looked at the 2005 trials when we were so much younger than everyone else in the field.

We played a good game and won to push our record to 4–1.

That afternoon following the McDonald game, Greg Ewasko, the head ice maker, came up to me and said he was thinking about touching up the rocks—sandpapering the bottom to make them a little more gritty so they would have a bit more curl.

I told him I thought we had enough curl on the ice, but Greg told me that to get that he had been having to nip too much of the pebble. When you do that, it makes the ice feel very flat and almost sticky to slide on.

That's not a great surface for my hip. It causes more discomfort and pain. I knew that if he kept the ice that way, it was not going to help me. But at the same time, if he sharpened the rocks, it would open up more of a window for teams with great sweeping. If they could flare shots out to the broom, they could carve them back in. It takes away a little of the precision, which is an area that our team excels at.

It was a Catch-22 for us. We were damned if he did and damned if he didn't.

For the betterment of the ice and to put the best product on display for the fans, it was probably the right decision to do the rocks. Greg said that he wasn't going to sharpen them too aggressively.

But when I got on the ice the next day, the first rock I threw curled six and a half feet. Before that we had been at four and a half feet, maybe five, which suited our team and suited our style. Six and a half feet was not going to be conducive to us playing really well.

That Wednesday turned out to be a very dark day. We lost to Saskatchewan's Mike McEwen in our sixth game and then lost our final game to Brad Jacobs.

A lot of people will naturally want to talk about my last rock against Brad, where we had a shot to win and I didn't make it. With that loss, we finished tied in the standings with Dunstone, but because we had lost to him in the round robin, he held the tiebreaker and went to the playoff.

I threw that last shot exactly the way I wanted to.

As soon as we called "whoa" on the sweep, Mark picked up his broom and the rock curled an inch.

That was the difference between making it and not making it, between going to the playoff and going home.

It was just a freak thing. Maybe if we had kept our brooms down I would have made the shot. Maybe in a different situation we would have taken the brooms up and the rock would have curled a half inch instead of an inch.

Everything was going through my head in that moment. I was angry and frustrated.

Either we didn't quite get the line call right or we didn't quite get the broom in the right spot and we missed by a hair.

I thought about all of that in the dressing room after the game. I hadn't seen the team so disappointed and upset in a long time.

The hard part of the Olympic trials is that you work for four years to get there, and there's only one winner. The last time, in 2022, we were on the right side of it and we walked away proud and happy. But if you go back to 2017 when, I think, we were by far the best team in the world and ended up losing in the semifinal, it was a dark time for us that went on for weeks if not months. That was the last time I had felt the same level of emotion and disappointment.

The conversation among us in the dressing room was tough. Brendan thought that even when we made contact, we had the shot—that's how close we were. That was actually hard for me to hear.

Looking back over the whole competition, we were all apologetic for one moment or another that could have changed things, whether it was that last shot or another one earlier in the week.

We changed into our street clothes and went out for a couple of beers and some pizza and the mood lightened a little. But it was still pretty sombre.

It started to sink in that this was my last chance to get to the Olympics as a competitor, and it definitely wasn't the way I had wanted that part of my life to end. Any time you miss your last shot and lose an event, whether you threw it great or not, it's hard to wash it away because you don't have another opportunity or another game to make up for it and create a better memory.

We stayed in Halifax for a couple more days and did some stuff with our families. On a few occasions we got together as a team and reflected more on what we did right and what we did wrong, what we could have done differently.

I thought about the personnel changes that we made on the team. Was it the right decision to not play as many events during the season as we normally would? Announcing my retirement—was that the right decision?

I questioned everything we had done over the last four years that might have had a negative impact on our performance at the trials. I was racking my brain, giving myself a really hard time on some of the key decisions and some of those key moments that could have made a difference.

But as I got further away from the loss, the more I decided that there wasn't much I would change. And I began to realize that maybe it wasn't about any of that.

I had to be honest with myself.

We weren't the best team there that week. We weren't at the level we needed to be at for the trials. It wasn't for lack of effort. It wasn't for lack of training or lack of will. We were just a step or two below where I believe we should have been, given the talent we have.

Even if I had made that shot against Team Dunstone and we had won that game, it would have been an uphill battle to go any further. If I'd made that shot, we would still have had to play Mike McEwen in the semifinals, and for the last couple of years Mike's had our number. He's always played really well against us.

And if we had managed to get past him, we would still have had to beat Jacobs twice. Seeing the way that those guys were playing, that would have been a daunting task. It's not like that shot lost us the chance to go to the Olympics. It certainly didn't help. But I know we would still have had a pretty tough road after that.

What I struggled with later wasn't so much that we lost.

It was the realization that for the first time in at least twelve years, I wasn't the best player out there.

I had always thought that if I played as well as I could, we were guaranteed to win. The stats and the data and the analytics all backed that up. I believed I was the best player in the world, and the numbers said the same thing.

Our team had won six Briers, Olympic gold and bronze, and fifteen Grand Slams. Nobody could argue with the results.

But at those trials, even if I was first in stats among the skips, I didn't feel that way.

It wasn't just that last shot.

All week, I had to invest so much mentally and physically just to draw out what I did. I remember saying to Krista that playing felt like hard work. It wasn't fun. I had to do everything I could just to stay focused so I could give my best on every shot.

Looking back, I'm super proud of what I achieved during the trials and I was pretty happy with every single rock that I threw. There might have been two rocks throughout the week that I'd love to have back that I didn't throw as well as I wanted.

But to do all of that and finish fourth, I'm just not used to that.

I guess it just wasn't meant to be.

The time following the trials was for licking our wounds. I don't think any of us had a desire to go out and throw rocks. We needed a little while to recover, to get mentally and emotionally past it, and then come back and realize we still have a pretty big event on the horizon.

I'm hoping we can correct course at the Brier in St. John's.

We did play better at the trials than we had all season—and were better than we'd been at any point since Brendan joined the team. That gives us some hope. And we still have a few months to devote to what we need to work on.

It's not as easy as just flipping the switch and saying, "Okay, now we focus on the Brier." Some grieving has to happen after a major loss. That's normal. We have all been through this before.

Even when you come back from the Olympics and you've been successful—in 2006 when we won the gold or 2022 when we won the bronze—we returned home with medals in hand but there was still a bit of a letdown that had to happen. We had built this thing up for four years, everything we had done had been leading to that moment, and then it was over and you're asking yourself, "Okay, so what do I do tomorrow?"

We've got the Grand Slam next week in Saskatoon. We'll have a team meeting before we get on the plane and regroup and put a plan in place.

I don't want to say I don't care about that event. It's going to be my last Grand Slam and I want to play well. But I'm going to cut myself and our team some slack.

With the age that we're at (ranging from forty-five to thirty-four), with my decision to retire, with Mark's decision looming about whether he is going to retire or keep playing after this season, it's understandable that we might go out there and not be 100 percent engaged.

We will still go through the proper process and do the right things. But if we're not as mentally sharp as we should be, I think we need to extend ourselves just a little bit of grace.

10

BUILDING THE PERFECT TEAM

There's no exact formula for putting together a curling team. Obviously, skill is a big factor, but personalities matter almost as much. Over the course of a season, members of a team spend more time together off the ice than on the ice. Trying to find the right dynamic where four players feel comfortable with each other isn't so simple.

I've been in situations where it's worked on the ice and it hasn't worked off the ice, and I've been in situations where it's worked great off the ice but it just hasn't worked on the ice. As much effort as you put into building a team and working with guys, sometimes it's just the luck of the draw. You don't know what it's going to be like until you do it.

I always want to start with four guys who get along. When you're away from your family and friends, it's important to enjoy the people you're around. Being together for upwards of two hundred days of the year is a test, and if you're stuck with someone you don't like, no matter how great a player they are, it can become unbearable.

I've made some personnel decisions over the course of my career that have been widely panned because we were playing well and that's all that people saw. But I knew that my relationship with a player, or one teammate's with another, wasn't working, even if no one on the outside understood that. All they saw was the product on the ice.

I have been able to brush off that criticism because I've known what was really going on. In some cases, there have been some pretty significant things happening behind the scenes that I didn't want to share in public. That kind of stuff has to stay within a team. More than once I've been tempted to say, "If you only knew what was really going on, you'd agree with me." But you just can't do that, out of fairness to the other players.

When a team breaks up, it's usually about relationships—something happens, or multiple somethings happen, and it's just time for a change. That was the case when we cut Jamie Korab in 2007. We were fresh off an Olympic gold medal and we had just lost the Brier final. People were shocked.

The reality was that off the ice, our team wasn't working as well as it had in years past. The dynamic within the team was completely different than what it was before the Olympics. We weren't gelling as a unit, and when that happens you've got to weigh the pros and cons of what you're doing on the ice against what's happening off the ice. There was also a personality conflict between Jamie and Mark Nichols. Mark finally said, "It's him or it's me," and there wasn't really any other choice to make.

More rarely, changes are made purely because of on-ice performance. Before Russ Howard came on the team in 2005, we had Keith Ryan, who just wasn't curling at the level we needed. He wasn't a bad guy and he fit in with us on a personal basis. But we were getting 75 percent out of him when we needed 85 or 90 percent, and we didn't feel he could raise his game that much.

Another move that a lot of people didn't understand was when we let Randy Ferbey go in 2011. Off the ice, I loved Randy. He was a fun guy to be around. Good stories. Kept things pretty loose.

He had much more of an old-school approach to curling than I did. I was very focused on fitness, whereas Randy was very social.

After a game, he needed to go to the Patch or to whatever the party was attached to the event we were competing in. That's how he got himself energized. But that was so different from the rest of us.

For a little while we partied right along with him—and I have to admit, it was a lot of fun—but on the ice, it just wasn't working. We were not playing anywhere near our capabilities. And so we had to move away from that relationship.

A few years later, I went to the Brier with Geoff Walker and two young players, Adam Casey and Ryan Fry.

Ryan was by far the best player at the 2012 Brier. An all-star. And then a couple weeks later, we cut him. Everybody was shocked, but if they'd known the whole story, they wouldn't have been. Off the ice, it just wasn't working. The dynamic wasn't there. Geoff and Adam weren't comfortable with Fry on the team. And there were a couple of very serious breaches of trust that I won't detail here. Suffice it to say that for the good of the team, I had no choice but to cut Ryan.

And then there was the Adam Casey decision in 2014. That was an interesting one because we were working so well both on and off the ice. Our team then was me, Geoff, Adam, and Brett Gallant. We reached a couple of Grand Slam finals and were competitive, but we just weren't taking that next step.

And then I found out that Mark Nichols was coming back to Newfoundland after having moved to Manitoba and playing for a couple of years there with Jeff Stoughton. I thought we could still improve as a team and that Mark's experience and our long relationship would be a help to us. It would mean I wasn't the only veteran in what was otherwise a really young group. The way I thought about it, adding Mark was a no-brainer. But who was I going to drop?

Geoff was playing lead and he had become one of the best in the world, so he was staying.

That left Brett and Adam.

It was right after the Brier, which meant we still had a few weeks left in the season. I told the others on the team that Mark was going to be joining us and one of them was going to be staying while the other would have to go. The decision, I said, would be based on how they curled over that final month and a half.

To be honest, Adam completely out-curled Brett. It wasn't even close. He handled the pressure to perform so well. But Mark wanted Brett on the team because he knew him better and felt that his personality was a better fit. And my priority was bringing Mark back.

That left me having to tell Adam that, even though he had clearly outplayed Brett, he was out.

Adam handled it with class, as he always did. But it tore me apart. It was one of my toughest moments as a skip, and I feel guilty about it to this day.

It's impossible to argue with our results over the following eight years. But I did feel better once we had Adam back in the fold as our fifth. He is one of the smartest people you'll ever meet, and someone I really rely on for advice. He's been a good friend, and is someone I've confided in—including my thoughts on retiring.

I do want to share a funny story about Adam.

There was a point when he, Geoff, and Brett were on the team when I wanted to share some of the administrative responsibilities and take a little bit of the workload and pressure off myself. Adam offered to take on booking our travel.

We had a competition coming up in Basel, Switzerland, and he took care of the flights and the accommodations. On the way over we had no issues; we flew into Zurich and then took a train up to Basel. But when I looked at the itinerary, I saw that Adam had booked us on a flight from Zurich to Geneva, with an overnight stay, then flights from Geneva to Toronto, Toronto to Montreal, Montreal to Halifax, and finally Halifax to St. John's. I was a bit frustrated by the amount of time it was going to take to get home, and we only saved a hundred bucks over a direct flight from Zurich to Toronto and then on to St. John's.

We also had to pay for a hotel in Geneva for the night. When we arrived, Adam told us that the hotel was right next door—close enough to walk, which would save us a few francs in taxi fare. As always, we were operating on a pretty tight budget.

We left the airport and started walking . . . and walking. We walked for two hours through an industrial section of town with no sign of the hotel. Finally, we gave up, walked back to the airport, and jumped in a cab. It turned out that the hotel Adam had booked was in Geneva, *France*, not Geneva, Switzerland. Although the border was close by, the hotel was in the wrong country and nowhere near the airport.

When we finally got to the hotel it was like something out of a horror movie. Outside it had a flickering fluorescent sign where all the letters weren't working. I got into my room and sat down on the bed and the mattress was so flimsy that it folded up around me.

I decided immediately that I wasn't staying there. Geoff and I hopped into a cab and found another hotel, but Adam had too much pride to do that. "No, I'm staying here," he said. "It's fine." Brett stayed with him.

The next day we met Adam and Brett at the airport, and you could tell right away that they didn't get a very good night's rest. And Brett kept scratching himself. You couldn't help but think about bedbugs.

That was the end of Adam booking our travel.

What happened with E.J. Harnden in 2024 was a little different because the change took place in the middle of a season, after we had some great results with him on the team. Naturally, it caused a big stir in the curling world.

When you're on the outside and the announcement comes out about a change in a team lineup, all the armchair quarterbacks make comments based on 10 percent of the facts, not the 90 percent that actually underlie the decision.

We had just come off winning two Briers. E.J. had worked his ass off for us, but we just didn't do a good enough job of incorporating him into our team.

Change usually happens because there's one player who is on an island by himself. When the other three are together, all you end up talking about is the guy who isn't there: "Why is he not a part of this? Why is he not engaging?" Sometimes the split is two and two, but usually it's three and one. It can be exhausting trying to find a solution.

That was the experience we had with E.J. towards the end. We wanted to make it work, but he just kept disengaging and going off on his own. If we lost and we had a shitty game, the guys would go out and have a great dinner and have some laughs, which helped us get over the disappointment. A lot of the time it was only the three of us going out. We would have to discuss the fact that E.J. wasn't there and then wait until we saw him the next day to talk about the game. That's the kind of thing that makes tough seasons tougher, when your team isn't firing on all cylinders.

We got to the end of the 2023–24 season with E.J., and even though we won the Brier, the three of us kind of hemmed and hawed about what we should do. We consulted with Curling Canada and talked to all of our advisors. We decided to try to keep the team together the next season and make some changes, accommodating E.J. a bit more.

It wasn't big stuff. For instance, the three of us preferred to stay in hotels on the road but E.J. wanted to be in an Airbnb, so in the interest of keeping the team together we agreed to do what E.J. wanted to do.

We tried to make him as comfortable as we could, but in the end it still didn't work. The three of us talked about our options, and we exhausted all things we thought we could do to make E.J. a better teammate. We realized that we weren't going to get any more out of him. And that's when we decided that our only choice was to make a change.

Looking back on it now, I think that E.J. must have been comfortable playing with his brother Ryan for the fifteen years in Northern Ontario before he came to us and we could never recreate that same level of support. At the end of the day, your brother can say whatever he wants to you, but you know he's still going to love you afterwards.

We were teammates, but we weren't brothers. It's not the same, and I think to play his best, E.J. needed his brother there. (It's no surprise that after he left us, he rejoined Ryan as part of Matt Dunstone's team.)

The other factor was that we found out Brendan Bottcher had suddenly become available, and we knew that a player as talented as he is wasn't going to be on the open market for very long. We had to make a pre-emptive move before another team snapped him up. I admit I dreaded having to tell E.J. that we were making the move. It's the part of being a skip that I like the least. It's like a relationship breakup—you say, "It's not you, it's me," but they don't hear that, and I understand why.

Having that conversation with E.J. was brutally difficult.

It was a risk making the change mid-season because it normally takes two or three years for a team to come together, and the first few months with a new player are nearly always rocky. We experienced that with Brendan. We didn't necessarily take a step forward right away. But our hope was that during the season we would get better as he became more comfortable with us and we became more comfortable with him.

So what does it take to make a great curling team?

Early in my career, I was guilty of trying to put the four best players together and assuming that's all it took to make the best team. But there is so much more involved in assembling a team.

It comes down to the players' work ethic and commitment and the personalities. If you have one guy who's not pulling his weight and working as hard as the others, no matter how talented he is, that's going to wreck a team. We've had some great players over the years who didn't work that hard, and it created an underlying animosity. Even though they might have been the most talented, shooting great numbers, the resentments build up.

You can usually tell when it's not going to work. But I've been in situations where you think guys are going to gel and they just never do. It's not science. There's some guesswork involved. If you try someone out and the team doesn't mesh, you have to either try to fix it or go looking for a better fit.

There's so much to learn and so much that you can only figure out after you've gone through high-pressure moments together. I've been in situations where someone is a great player and seems to be a great teammate. Then all of a sudden we reach a final and I get in the hack and the guy says to me: "We can't miss this one heavy." So then I can't help but think about missing the rock heavy before I even throw. That's not going to work. You can't suddenly say that to me when the pressure is on.

Off the ice, it's a whole lot easier if guys are friends, but I don't think that's always absolutely necessary. I remember the Kevin Martin teams from around 2008–10. They had the highest ceiling of any curling team that I've ever seen, but they didn't do too much off the ice as a foursome. Kevin was older than the other three guys and they didn't often hang out.

When we were at our peak, our teams have enjoyed being around each other off the ice. We liked having conversations over dinner. It made everything more enjoyable than doing it the other way, when you're just going about your business and playing the game but don't have much of a relationship beyond that.

It's great to go out together and shit on each other. If you did something wrong, you'd hear about it all weekend in a lighthearted way. It was fun—especially if you weren't the one being messed with.

We are on the road for sixteen weeks of the year, and together for sixteen hours a day. We share hotel rooms or rented houses. We don't get much of a break from each other. When you add it up, we probably spend as much or more time with our teammates than we do with our wives.

You don't have to be the best of friends, but you have to trust each other.

There are natural ebbs and flows during a season. You're going to have good games, bad games, good events, bad events. The down times are so much tougher when you don't have a team that gets along. It can make you feel like you're on your own.

I can't tell you how it works for everybody else, but I can tell you about what I think was our best team. It was the one we had from 2014 to 2022 with Mark, Geoff, Brett, and me. We had as much success as any rink in history, and I think that's the closest I've come to achieving what I've attempted to achieve for most of my career, which was to put the best curling team, ever, on the ice.

I started skipping when I was fifteen, which was only a couple of years after I started playing, and I have skipped ever since. (The only time I wasn't in the house was the year we won the 2006 Olympics with Russ Howard, where I was still throwing last rocks but he was calling the first part of the game.) My skill set and my personality led me there. You have to be in charge, you have to be able to manage your team, you have to be able to think through the game, and you have to be able to handle the big moment.

There are some successful teams on which the skip is very easygoing and probably doesn't make all the decisions. But that's not the norm.

If you're a skip, it's your name that's attached to the rink. Naturally you want control. I think that's only fair and reasonable. You're the one who gets all the blame if things don't go well and you're the one who often gets more credit than you deserve.

A skip has to be like a closer in baseball, a shooting guard in the NBA, a quarterback in the NFL, and a little bit like a goalie in hockey. It is the position where all of the pressure lands. You can play an absolutely perfect game, but if your skip misses that last shot, you lose.

I have always wanted to be the guy in that position. I've had offers to join some great teams over the years with great players. But I'd rather be the guy throwing the last rock. To be a good skip, I think you have to have that mentality.

You also have to be a good strategist. I grew up playing chess and loved thinking through the moves and countermoves. I've played some poker, too, which involves understanding odds. I love math, I love numbers, I love calculation.

The bottom line is that I think you either have it in you to be a skip or you don't. There aren't many players who develop into one.

Over the years, I learned to be a good leader through a lot of hard work, and a lot of listening to people who told me how I needed to improve.

For our team to work, the three other guys have to respect me in that role, and I have had to give them enough leeway and support to become the best at what they did.

One of the reasons that the 2014–22 version of our team was so successful was that I allowed Brett and Geoff the freedom to go out and fail—and I put them in situations where they failed quite often. I gave them a lot of responsibility. I would come down and ask them what weight they thought I should throw in a certain path. Even if I sometimes knew it was probably not the right weight, I would trust them and I'd throw it. Whether I made or missed the shot, they learned from the experience.

I tried to be as patient as I could. Earlier in my career I would become angry or frustrated with teammates if they made the wrong call. It was Toby and our sports psychologist at the time, Kyle Paquette, who stressed to me that I had to change. Brett and Geoff were new on tour then, they were new to curling at the elite level, and they were going to make mistakes.

I had gone through that same learning curve earlier in my career and I didn't want to go through it again, but I was in a situation where it was necessary if we were going to get better. Eventually Brett and Geoff realized that if they fucked up, we were going to talk about it and analyze what happened, but I wasn't going to come down too hard on them. They learned from their mistakes and they got more comfortable, and eventually they became two of the best of all time at judging rocks, judging weight, and judging paths.

Sometimes you see teams where the skip is overpowering. And I admit I was guilty of that early in my career—what I said was the law. But with Mark, Brett, and Geoff, we created a dynamic that allowed for four opinions, four viewpoints, which is a whole lot better than just one.

It's not a democracy. Ultimately if a decision has to be made, it's on me, 100 percent, and I take ownership of it.

But it's also not a dictatorship (though there are some skips who operate that way). It's not "What I say goes."

Off the ice, when it comes down to how the team functions from a business standpoint or a logistical standpoint, the guys rely on me. I will hear them out, but ultimately my decision is final. On the ice, I value feedback. When the guys speak up, I listen—especially with Mark and Geoff, because they normally don't say a lot. It's a good, healthy dynamic.

The only situation where what I say goes is when we are talking about my shots. Otherwise, there are four votes on the ice. If it is one of the other guys' shots and it's three against one about what we should do, we will generally go with the majority or with the guy who is shooting. Very rarely, if ever, will I overrule three guys—I honestly can't remember a situation where it's happened.

Beyond the skip, I think different people are cut out for the different roles on a team.

Lead is the most challenging position in the sport. It's very repetitive, playing the same sort of shots over and over again to start a game. A good lead has to be someone who can handle that routine and who is happy not being in the spotlight. Often on a telecast, they don't even show a lead's rocks, so they can be a little forgotten.

But they are such a crucial part of being successful on the ice. If you don't have a great lead, you're not going to win, period. You have to find someone who is willing to do the mundane work of throwing draws and guards and who excels at it.

That's Geoff Walker, who is one of the best leads to ever play the game. He has never craved attention, and he's been incredible at doing his job for a long time. I have a huge amount of respect for him. He's one of my favourite teammates, ever.

Throwing second stone also involves a bit of repetition, but you do get the chance to play a few more different shots than you do as a lead. We've had some really interesting personalities at second stone over the years, and a big challenge for our team has been finding the right one.

We had it for a long time with Brett Gallant. He often offered a different perspective on the ice. There were times when I changed my mind on a shot based on what he was saying.

And then there's the third, who is normally the second-in-command, a kind of vice-skip. But on our team, Mark Nichols really isn't that. He's a pretty chill guy who doesn't crave attention and who just wants to go out and do his job really well.

What Mark does better than anyone else is manage me. He knows when to say something and when to stay quiet. He knows that if I'm going good and in the zone, he should just put the broom down and let me do what I do.

I've played with some other people in that position who will plant a seed of doubt in a pressure situation, and that's rattled me. But Mark knows to just let me go. There are other times when he senses that I'm not as confident as I should be, and then he'll subtly steer me towards playing the right shot. That's a really good skill in a third.

Those three guys were the best version of our team. We were together for eight years, and we were at our absolute peak from 2016 to 2018, especially from the 2017 worlds to the 2018 Brier. We didn't lose many games during that stretch, and if we did lose it was because another team played extremely well against us and they earned it.

Our team became known for a kind of peskiness, a resilience. If we got down early you knew we were coming back and you knew you were going to have to make the last shot. We never got blown out of games.

We had the 2018 Olympic trials during that stretch, and it was one of the rare times when we lost—to a red-hot Mike McEwen in the semifinal. It was one of the better games I've seen a skip play against us. Mike all but single-handedly beat us.

That's not to say we would have won the final for sure. I definitely don't want to suggest that. But I will always believe that we should have won the trials and gone on to the 2018 Games in South Korea.

I tend to remember the losses more than the wins. Not so much events, but I definitely remember individual games that our team lost and shots I missed more than shots made and games won. Those are the moments that stick with me. And the 2018 Olympic trials is the event I feel worst about. There were some Briers that I think we had a good chance to win and didn't, some finals that we lost, but we weren't necessarily the best team at the time.

Whereas at those trials, we were without a doubt the best team in the world. We were beating everyone. We should have won and didn't. We walked away from that experience with nothing other than some extra motivation to go out and defend our title at the 2018 Brier in Regina.

In the history of Canadian curling there have been some interesting connections between Newfoundland and Saskatchewan. Regina is where Jack MacDuff won the first Brier for our province in 1976.

Sam Richardson, a legendary curler who won four Briers for Saskatchewan back in the 1960s, was the driver for that Newfoundland team in the '76 tournament, and they always said he played a role in their success.

It was our first time playing a Brier in Regina. (The previous time it was held there was 2006, but we were at the Olympics then.) Mark and I made a point of having our picture taken with the great Ernie Richardson, Sam's brother, who was the skip of that famous Saskatchewan team.

We started out playing as well as we played at the world championships the year before, where we finished undefeated and won every game pretty handily.

There was only one stumble. On the Tuesday we had a morning game scheduled against Brendan Bottcher and Team Alberta. The night before, one of our sponsors took us out for a nice steak dinner at a famous place called The Diplomat. No booze, but we definitely had some big steaks and some serious, heavy meals.

We woke up the next morning feeling like we were moving in slow motion. During the game we were flat, and Brendan ended up beating us.

That's when we made the decision that we were no longer going to eat steaks anytime we were competing. To this day that's still our team policy.

When we got to the playoffs, the other three teams were Brad Jacobs, John Epping, and Brendan, who at that time was still fairly new on the scene.

We played John in the one-two game and won pretty easily. He had a younger team, and I don't think they played as well as they could have.

That put us into the final.

We knew we would be playing either John, Brad, or Brendan, and our biggest concern of those three was obviously Brad, because he had one of the top teams in the country. They had won at the Brier, the Olympic trials, and several Slams.

But then Brad lost the three-four game to Brendan. We were on our way to the rink to practise when we heard the result. That meant that John and Brendan were left. From a statistical standpoint, and knowing how we had performed throughout the week, we felt we were in pretty good shape.

I remember thinking, *This is ours to win. We've just got to go out and do our job.*

So many times over the course of my career, when I've become a little too cocky, it has come back to bite me. But our team was just so good that season. After Brendan beat John in the semifinal, we took control of the final and didn't look back. Brendan never really pushed us, and even though the score was close, we didn't have to force the issue.

Coming into the last end, we were one up with the hammer. Brendan's team played a really good end and had shot rock that was just biting the button.

With my final shot I had to draw the button to win the Brier.

Of course, if I had missed the shot, we would have gone to an extra end, so we had a bit of a cushion. But still, it was a draw to the button to win in front of however many thousand fans had packed the Brandt Centre.

I remember letting the shot go and thinking, *That's as good as I could throw a rock*. No matter what happened, I was satisfied—which was a lot different from how I had felt the year before in St. John's. I thought I had made a good shot then, too, but I couldn't be sure because I was so nervous.

This time when I let go, I was calm and confident and thought we were going to have to mess up pretty good to miss. The guys swept perfectly and the rock covered the pin.

Jeff Stoughton had said to me once, "Even if you win a Brier, people can still say it was a fluke. But when you win two, it's no fluke."

And now we had two—and two in a row. I think that win put our team on another level. We weren't a one-hit wonder. We had been dominant all season, we had been dominant throughout that Brier (other than that one game), and we controlled the final.

We were on top of the world.

11

THE PANDEMIC

In the fall of 2020, Newfoundland was part of the "Atlantic bubble." During that phase of the COVID pandemic, people living on the island and in the Maritime provinces were allowed to move freely within the region. It meant that the team could at least play a little. But we all assumed that because of all the restrictions in the rest of Canada, the season was going to be cancelled—which is why I decided to begin a full-year MBA remotely at Queen's University. I figured that I wasn't going to be curling for who knew how long, so I might as well take the opportunity to advance my education. I knew that my curling career at that point was on the back nine, and here was a chance to prepare for my life afterwards.

Soon after I registered at Queen's, word came that the curling season was going to go ahead after all, with the events played in a single location behind closed doors in Calgary. We were going to have a couple of Grand Slams, the Brier, the Scotties, and mixed doubles. I was going to have to be in Alberta for a minimum of four events and, if we won the Brier and qualified for the world championships, even longer.

Because of the COVID rules in Newfoundland, which required entering a fourteen-day quarantine when you returned to the province, we couldn't go home between events. We would have to stay out west the whole time. So we rented a house in Calgary where our team could live between competitions and then check into the designated bubble hotel when it was time to play.

It was a great thing for curling that we found a way to keep playing. There weren't many sporting events taking place during the early part of the pandemic, so there was extra interest when we came on TV.

But the experience was tough on the players—and especially on us. Entertaining yourself when you're confined to a house or hotel away from your family for weeks at a time was a real challenge. There's a video somewhere online of Mark walking ten thousand steps in his room—that was his workout. Eventually we were allowed to go as far as the parking lot, but we still couldn't leave the hotel property.

Those months became like *Groundhog Day*, going through the same routine over and over again. The events had different names, the Grand Slams and the Brier, but they were played in the same building on the same ice. We went to the same dressing room. It felt like we were on repeat, over and over again.

I struggled in that environment. I admit that when I'm competing, I'm a bit of a curling attention-whore. In my normal life, I'm not like that at all. I don't need to be the centre of attention at a party. I'd rather sit in the corner and be by myself or with a small group. But when I'm competing, I want people to watch me. I want people to cheer.

I remember playing one game where I was on fire, making every shot—in-offs, run doubles, draws to the side of the button. Then I capped it off by making a really difficult raised double takeout. I gave my teammates a big fist pump. And then I heard a toilet flush from underneath the stands. That's how quiet and empty the building was.

We struggled as a team. There were a couple of Grand Slams where we played okay, but we didn't even make the playoffs at the Brier.

My only real success during that strange season came when I played mixed doubles with Manitoba's Kerri Einarson. When people list my curling accomplishments, winning the Canadian championship with Kerri in 2021 is almost never included. I remember it vividly and it's one I'm very proud of, especially considering the extraordinary circumstances.

Mixed doubles is a very athletic, fast-moving game. It keeps the fans engaged, there are always rocks in play, and a three- or four-point lead can disappear in a flash. I wish it had been around earlier in my career. By the time I started playing I was in my late thirties and had my hip injury, so I really couldn't go for it the way I would have liked.

Because of the pandemic, that was probably the best mixed doubles field that Canada has ever had—or ever will have—at a national championship. All the top players were already stuck in the bubble. The attitude was, why not put a team together and give it a shot? We might as well curl instead of watching everybody else curl.

Marc Kennedy played with Val Sweeting. Mark Nichols played with Briane Meilleur. I reached out to Selena Njegovan to see if she wanted to play, but it turned out that she had already committed to team up with Reid Carruthers. And then Kerri asked me if I wanted to form a team with her, and I said yes immediately. She is a great player and I felt that we'd get along well.

Kerri really hadn't played any mixed doubles at that point. I'd played in the Olympic trials back in 2018 with Val Sweeting and had some success—we lost in the final to John Morris and Kaitlyn Lawes. But outside of that I had only competed a couple of times. And Kerri and I are two skips who couldn't really sweep and two players who didn't even know the mixed doubles rules all that well. We were literally learning as we went along.

In our first game we played Jennifer Jones and Brent Laing, and we were still trying to figure it out. We were making mistakes and hitting rocks when we weren't allowed to be hitting them and we got beaten up pretty good.

We lost another one of our early games, but then we started to understand how to work together. Kerri was playing very well. She shot the lights out and it was fun to ride her coattails. And from a strategic standpoint I was starting to understand when was a good time to be aggressive and when was a good time to bail. We got on a pretty good roll by the end of the round robin.

In the first round of playoffs we were matched against Brittany Tran and Aaron Sluchinski from Alberta. After beating them, we faced Jennifer Jones and Brent Laing again. This time it was a completely different game. We scored five in the first, stole three in the second end and went on to win 11–2.

We lost to Kadriana Sahaidak and Colton Lott from Manitoba 8–5 in page seeding game, then we beat Kirk Muyres and Laura Walker, who had gone undefeated through the round robin. That put us into the semifinal against John Morris and Danielle Schmiemann. I remember making a couple of pretty awesome shots in that game and we ended up winning comfortably.

In the final we played Colton Lott and Kadriana Sahaidak (now his wife), and we dominated the game and won pretty easily.

We were the Canadian mixed doubles champions, and we thought that was it for us because the pandemic was still raging on.

But afterwards we were having a few drinks with Scott Pfeifer, who was the Canadian team lead for the mixed doubles teams, and he said that it looked like there was going to be a world championship for mixed doubles after all. The plan was to play towards the end of April in Aberdeen, Scotland.

I remember thinking, *Are you serious?* We hadn't thought we were going to be travelling anywhere.

Both Kerri and I had been in Calgary for upwards of two and

a half months by that point. We were both anxious to get home and relax.

I was at least able to fly back to Newfoundland for two weeks—which I had to spend in isolation up at our cabin. But Kerri had to stay in the bubble to play the women's world championship.

As soon as that was done, she got on a plane to Aberdeen, while I took off for Scotland without ever really seeing my family.

When we got there, we had to isolate for five days before the event started. After that there was another bubble. We weren't allowed to leave the hotel grounds other than to take a bus to the curling club where the competition was being held.

I never got to see any of Aberdeen or even eat in a restaurant because we had to have all of our meals at the hotel. Coming off the weeks of isolation in Calgary, it was a mental and emotional challenge. Both Kerri and I were fed up and tired of being away from our families for so long. We were both so exhausted and so lonely. We wanted that event to be over as quickly as possible.

But we also knew that we had to earn enough points to get Canada into the mixed doubles event at the Olympics. At the world championship, your finish determines how many points your country earns toward qualifying. Over a couple of years, the countries that have the most points get a direct berth in the Olympics. We knew we needed to make the playoffs to make sure that Canada had a spot in the Games, and that became our number one goal.

We struggled quite a bit over there. For some reason, we just couldn't find the game that we had in Calgary. We couldn't get comfortable with the draw weight. It became one of those weeks where we had to grind through and try to get as much out of it as we could.

We ended up going 7–2 in the round robin. It wasn't a pretty 7–2, but it was good enough to make the playoffs and achieve our goal.

And then we came up against a couple of really good teams. We lost to Bruce Mouat and Jennifer Dodds in the semifinal and then we were beaten by Oskar Eriksson and Almida de Val in the bronze medal game.

When I came home after the world championships, I had to isolate for another two weeks before I could be in the same room with Krista and the girls. I had entered the bubble towards the end of February and I finally cleared my last isolation on June 16.

It was a long, long haul.

By the fall of 2021, it finally felt like things were getting back to normal. We won the Olympic trials for the Beijing Olympics, and then I went to Kingston to spend a week working on my MBA at Queen's. It was the first time I had met my classmates in person, and I really enjoyed it.

Then some rumours started spreading around campus that there was a COVID outbreak from a new variant called Omicron. I immediately hightailed it out of Kingston and did the rest of the session over Zoom. With the Olympics coming up, I wasn't taking any chances.

By the time I got back to St. John's, it became pretty clear that we were at the beginning of another COVID wave. Our team went into semi-isolation, but we did have a short training camp in Newfoundland the week before Christmas where Geoff and our support staff flew in.

On Christmas Day, I was over at my mom and dad's house for our traditional supper. We had just finished our meal and were about to have dessert when I got a text from Geoff telling me that he had tested positive for COVID. And of course we had just spent that time in close contact with each other.

There was already a lot of talk that China wasn't going to let anyone into the country to compete if they had any trace of COVID in their system. Things got really scary. We were thinking Geoff might be barred from the Olympics and that there was clearly a chance the rest of us were also going to test positive and not be able to go.

On Boxing Day our team got on a call with Curling Canada and the Canadian Olympic Committee. We decided that our best option was to go into our own hyperintense bubble. We were going to go to B.C., find a house, rent a curling club, get away from everybody, focus on training—and make sure we did everything we could to stay away from COVID.

We travelled to B.C. on January 13, 2022—over three weeks away from Beijing. We found a farmhouse near Abbotsford and rented the Abbotsford Curling Club, which was closed because of COVID. Our time was spent practising a couple of times a day and otherwise hanging out at the house playing pool, cards, and video games as well as doing puzzles.

It was fun for a little while, but it got old really quick.

There was also a bit of internal drama taking place with our team.

A few weeks earlier, someone had come up to me at one of the Grand Slams and told me that Brett Gallant was going to be leaving and that he already had a new team lined up for the next season with Ben Hebert and a couple of other guys in Alberta. It didn't come as a huge shock. Brett's girlfriend was in Calgary, and it made sense that he might want to move out there to join her. But he certainly hadn't told us that.

It felt like it was a little too early in the season to address it, so I just filed that information away and we went on to play the Olympic trials.

Two days after the trials ended, we had a team meeting. I was about to head off to Kingston for my classes and I wanted to talk about what was going to happen with our team going forward. I didn't let on what I had been told.

"I don't care what you do next year or in the next quadrennial," I told the guys. "I just want us to share and be open and be honest about what's going on. If you guys want to stay together, I'm more than happy for us to stay together."

We went around the room.

Mark and Geoff both said they were in. But Brett was noncommittal. I had given him an opportunity to tell us that he was leaving and he decided not to take it.

It's completely normal for guys to change teams, especially at the end of an Olympic cycle. We would have understood. We had been together for eight years. We all knew Brett was probably moving to Calgary. It made sense and we would have been cool with it.

But he chose not to come clean, and now we were locked up in a house together with me getting texts from other players who had heard Brett was leaving and wanted to join our team. My frustration continued to build.

I didn't force the issue with him. I didn't flat out ask him. I guess I didn't want to make it that blatant. But the door was open, and Brett chose not to say a word.

There was another member of our team who was part of the Abbotsford lockdown: our coach Jules Owchar, who by that point had been with us for several years, including the first three Brier wins.

Back in 2013, Kevin Martin asked me to be the fifth on his team at the trials leading up to the 2014 Olympics.

It had been a real disappointment that we didn't get to the trials with our own team, which was just starting to break out. But the pretrials event was stacked. Brad Jacobs was there, as were Jim Cotter and John Morris, who went on to lose the Brier final that season. There were only two spots open to go to the full Olympic trials and three or four really competitive teams.

We got to the A Final and lost to Morris, which meant that John qualified for the trials. Then we dropped the B Final to Brad Jacobs and were eliminated. At that point I felt I was the best player in the world and we had a team that was on the rise, but we just weren't good enough that week.

Almost immediately, I got the call from Kevin. He had been experiencing some back spasms throughout the year and had missed some games because of that. I think his team wanted a skip on board who could jump in and still make them competitive if Kevin couldn't go.

I happily agreed to do it. They were one of the favourites to go to the Olympics and it was a great opportunity for me to learn from Kevin and from that team.

Jules was coaching Kevin's team then. Every night after we played, I wound up in Kevin's room, having a few drinks, and Jules would always join us. (I probably drank more that week than I did at any point in my curling career, to be quite honest.) He was a coach at the Northern Alberta Institute of Technology, which is where he met Kevin. They had worked together for twenty years and developed a great relationship.

I immediately liked Jules's chill nature and admired his deep knowledge of the game.

Brad Jacobs wound up winning those trials and went on to take the gold medal in Sochi.

When Kevin decided to retire at the end of that season, I asked Jules if he would be interested in coaching our team. He said yes and would go on to have a huge impact on my career.

When we would go to an event we would drop Jules off at the rink at eight o'clock in the morning and pick him up after the last game of the night. If we were playing in the afternoon he would meet us there and then he would stick around and watch all the other games to learn as much as he could. He had the most unhealthy eating habits of any of us—he lived on arena hot dogs and donuts. There were often times when we would be going out for a nice supper, and he'd say, "No, I want to watch some games." He was a true rink rat.

We called Jules our "rock guru" because he loved to chart the stones and find the subtle differences in how they performed. If someone switched a rock in the fourth or fifth end, he'd make a note of it. By the time we got on a sheet, he could tell us which rocks had issues way before the other teams figured it out, which was a definite competitive advantage.

During our games, he was a real cool customer. When we got to the big moments, he never let us feel the pressure—and if he was feeling any himself, he sure didn't show it. I remember playing a Brier final in Ottawa in 2016 and looking over and seeing Jules resting his chin on his hand, almost like he was going to fall asleep. I was thinking, *Man, I'm not nearly as relaxed as you are.* That made me feel comfortable, and it was the same when we got to Brier semis or finals, and even at the Olympics.

Away from curling, Jules was a bit of a man of mystery, at least to us. He was a lot older than the rest of us, but we were never quite sure how much older. We used to ask him about what he was like when he was younger, but he never offered up much information.

To get into China, we had to fill out a huge amount of paperwork, and because Jules was up in age and super nervous about travelling during the pandemic, we took care of that for him to make sure all the forms were completed correctly. Geoff Walker filled out everything that was required for Jules's Olympic accreditation. But he didn't actually ask Jules for the information. He got it off of a Wikipedia page.

When we were at the Vancouver airport before flying to Tokyo and then on to Beijing, we looked at Jules's passport and realized that the information on his accreditation documents didn't line up. He was a couple of years older than Wikipedia said he was. And his first name wasn't Jules—it was Julius.

At the airport, we had to spend a couple of hours talking to the Canadian Olympic Committee and immigration to correct all his information so that we could get him into China.

♣

It was an incredible accomplishment getting back to the Olympics, but it turned out to be so different from what I had experienced in 2006.

In Italy, we were free to get out and see the country and to enjoy the culture, the people, and the food. But when we went to China, there was none of that.

When we landed at the airport in Beijing, the only way you'd have known the Olympics was happening was that there was a little bit of signage at the airport with the Olympic logo. As soon as we got off the plane, security pushed us along like cattle to get our COVID tests. It was all very regimented.

Once we had our negative tests, we were herded onto a bus. All the windows were covered by curtains, so we couldn't even see the city as we drove in.

We were let out at the athletes' village, and from that point on it was village-venue-village-venue for the rest of the Games. We weren't allowed to go outside of a secured perimeter. We didn't see any of the community.

We got to the rink and they had the Olympic rings on the walls, but when you looked up all you saw were thousands of empty seats. It was a cavernous building—the Water Cube, the same place they had used for aquatic competitions during the 2008 Summer Olympics, and it was rechristened the Ice Cube for the Winter Games. They had built scaffolding over the pool and put the ice on top of it. You walked past the hot tub where the divers went between dives and then turned a corner and suddenly you were standing on ice. Needless to say, I'd never been in a venue like that before.

We had been in the bubble for so long that we really needed the energy of a crowd to get us motivated. In Pinerolo in 2006, the atmosphere had been incredible. But in Beijing in the middle of a pandemic, it just wasn't there.

The ice was very straight and slow, which wasn't conducive to our style of play, and we struggled. We lost games to teams we shouldn't have lost to, and even when we won, some of them were games we didn't deserve to win.

But somehow we made it to the semifinal, where we were matched against Niklas Edin and his Swedish team and found ourselves one down with the hammer in the last end with a real chance to win.

Niklas got very fortunate on his last shot. For some reason, the rock curled more than it should have, then hit and stopped just in time to lie shot. That left me facing a really difficult raise double takeout that I might make one time out of ten.

I missed it by millimetres.

The second the rock stopped, I felt devastated, knowing that we weren't going to have a chance to play for gold.

The venue had screens set up where you could see your family watching back home. I remember coming off the ice and seeing my girls there and getting very emotional.

My instinct in that moment was that our Olympics were over. Gold medal or bust. We were there to win and we fell short. It's instinctual for an athlete.

But then we went back to the dressing room and had a really good conversation. I have to give a lot of credit to Marc Kennedy, who was our fifth. He had been on the Canadian team at the Olympics in 2018 that lost the semifinal and then lost the bronze medal game. Marc talked about how the biggest regret of his career was not coming out for that last game with more energy and more passion.

It struck a real chord with me. I didn't want to leave with any regrets from this experience. Our road to those Olympic games had been mentally, physically, and emotionally draining. If we could win a bronze medal, it would make it all worthwhile.

We came out in the bronze medal game and curled well—not a

Mark and I as we head to the 2022 Olympics in Beijing. We had to take so many precautions. (Courtesy of the author.)

Kerri Einarson and I after we won the 2021 Canadian Mixed Doubles Championships in the "Calgary bubble." (Courtesy of Michael Burns/Curling Canada.)

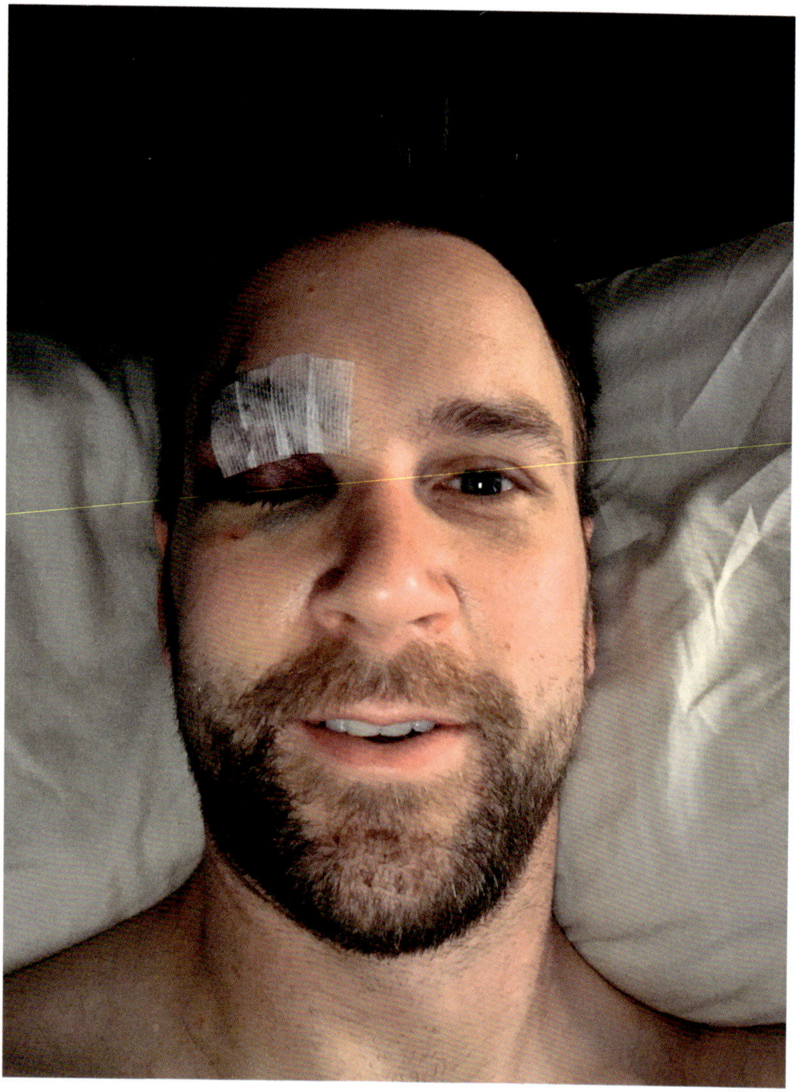

The day after I fell on my face in Truro during the Grand Slam in 2015. (Courtesy of the author.)

Toby McDonald, after we received our Gold Medal. He was as big a part of it as anyone. (Courtesy of the author.)

Me and the girls taking in batting practice before a Blue Jays game. (Courtesy of the author.)

The girls in their provincial jackets, and I am in my Canada jacket, at a photo shoot. A present for the grandparents. (Courtesy of Trevor Wragg.)

Watching Hayley playing Marissa at the U16 provincials. It was tough watching that one. (Courtesy of David Brophy.)

Krista and the girls with me after our second Brier win in Regina, Saskatchewan, in 2018. (Courtesy of the author.)

Proud moment when I passed Kevin Martin and Russ Howard for the most wins in Brier history as a skip. Finished with 198. (Courtesy of Michael Burns/Curling Canada.)

The Team! My teammates: Adam, Mark, Geoff, Jeff and Brendan, along with Kate, my friend and longtime massage therapist, and Krista, Hayley and Marissa. Couldn't have finished my career with a better group. Very grateful for their support and friendship. (Courtesy of the author.)

I was fortunate to play most of my career with Mark Nichols. We had a lot of success together. (Courtesy of Anil Mungal.)

Krista embracing me after my final game. It was a very emotional moment, and I'm so glad she was there. (Courtesy of Ryan Cooke.)

great game, but a good game considering the conditions—and beat John Schuster's U.S. team by three points.

To this day, I'm as proud of that bronze medal as I am of the gold. Looking back on both Olympic experiences, I know that a lot of things broke our way in 2006 and a lot of things tipped against us in 2022. It was an uphill climb. But we were still able to get the bronze, which was an incredible achievement.

We received our medals in the almost empty Ice Cube—a far cry from that crazy scene in Turin in front of thousands. In all there were maybe forty or fifty Canadian athletes and support staff there, plus about the same number from the other two countries. And no Ricky Martin concert.

When I looked down at that bronze medal, I was pretty damn proud of what we had overcome to get it. It remains one of the best moments of my career.

When I came home from the Olympics, family and friends were waiting to meet me when I got off the plane. We had a really nice evening celebrating.

I woke up the next morning to find someone at my front door serving me with legal papers.

It was a lawsuit filed against our team and Curling Canada by Team John Epping—John, Ryan Fry, Brent Laing, and Mathew Camm. They were claiming that we should not have been allowed entry to the upcoming Brier in Lethbridge as a wild-card team since Olympic curling teams had never participated in the Brier in the past because of the timing of the Games.

At that point we were number one in the Canadian team rankings, they were number two, and they were trying to make the case that they should have been given that spot ahead of us.

It was completely shocking. There was no precedent for it.

Instead of celebrating and relaxing after the Olympics, I spent the next day finding a lawyer and not knowing if we were going to be able to compete in the Brier—which was starting in five days. Talk about a buzzkill.

I got in touch with Curling Canada and we got all our ducks in a row and assembled the necessary documents.

And then Ryan made a mistake.

He accidentally cc'd everyone, including us, on a message to his lawyer in which he made it clear that what their team was really looking for was a financial settlement. They wanted to be paid off by Curling Canada in return for dropping the lawsuit.

Ryan later tried to walk back his comments, but that email made their real intentions clear.

A day before we were scheduled to leave for the Brier, an arbitrator threw out the suit. It never went public, and this is the first time I have ever talked about it.

I had missed my family so much during the eight weeks I was away from home before and during the Olympics that I decided to fly them to Lethbridge for the Brier.

Pandemic restrictions had loosened up in Canada, but COVID was still out there. Our team decided to take the same precautions that we had leading up to the Olympics—wearing masks, staying in, avoiding other teams, avoiding people in general. We wanted to be safe and we wanted to be able to perform.

The pressure of the Olympics was gone, the ice at the ENMAX Centre was the way we liked it, and we were way more comfortable. That showed in our play. We went undefeated heading into the last game of the round robin.

And then, halfway through that game, Mark came up to me and said, "Brad, I don't feel very good."

My first reaction was to brush it off. We were all physically rundown and still feeling the time change from China. We had dealt with the stress of the lawsuit and were now playing intense Brier games. It would be pretty normal not to feel 100 percent healthy in those circumstances.

I told Mark to get a good night's sleep. We had twenty-four hours before our next game and I was pretty sure that he'd be fine.

The next day was a sleep-in day because we weren't playing until the evening. So when Mark FaceTimed me at six in the morning, I knew it wasn't good news.

Even on the screen I could see that Mark looked awful. He told me that he'd been up all night with a fever of 103 and he was sweating like crazy. He had a headache, a really sore throat, and his voice was just about gone.

In other words, all the classic COVID symptoms.

The rule at the Brier was that if you tested positive, you couldn't compete. At the same time, though, there was no obligation for players to test. We had a decision to make.

Mark looked so bad that I knew he wasn't going to be fooling anybody. I told him to take the test, and that if it was positive, as I was sure it would be, we'd find a way to deal with it.

Of course, his test lit up right away.

I called Curling Canada, which connected me with a doctor and a nurse. My next step was to talk to the other guys on the team. We had decided not to bring a fifth man to the Brier—it was optional, and we had done fine without a fifth several times before. But in this instance, that decision backfired.

We were going to have to play with three for the rest of the competition—or at least we were if we still had three healthy players. We had been living in very tight quarters. Geoff had already had COVID, so we figured he had some immunity and was likely pretty safe. But Brett and I hadn't had COVID yet, so we were vulnerable. If one of us got sick, we'd be down to two players and would be disqualified from the Brier.

I felt okay. I had no symptoms. But by Saturday, heading into the playoffs, Brett was starting to feel a little off.

Because we had finished in first place in the round robin, we had a bit of a cushion—we could drop the first playoff game and not be eliminated. Playing with three, plus dealing with the shock of Mark not being there, we didn't play particularly well in that first game and we lost.

I like to think of what came next as an eff-you moment.

Mark was out, we were playing with three, we'd lost the first playoff game, and our Brier was going up in smoke.

That's when I thought, *Frig it.* Everybody was writing us off even though we had just won another Olympic medal, even though we were three-time champions. *Let's go out and prove them wrong.*

Our next game was against Colton Flasch and his Saskatchewan rink. We were playing the last end and were down by one. It looked like we were in a good position to score two and win the game. Then Colton made an incredible shot with his first rock. He hit and rolled behind a centre guard and it was completely buried. The only way for us to score two was to chase his rock and bump it out.

But the ice wasn't curling enough for that shot to be possible. Instead, I went back to something that I had practised a lot when I was younger. I would slide two feet off the broom on purpose and then sort of hook the stone around to create a wider arc.

I don't like to pull that shot out too often because it's not the easiest to execute and the odds of success are low. But they are a little higher for me than for most people because I've worked at it over the course of my career.

Halfway down the sheet, I knew I had found the slot. The guys swept the stone and it got by the guard by maybe a couple of millimetres, hit their rock, bumped it just out of play and then rolled to where we were lying two again. On TV it might have looked like just a normal chase around the guard, but from a curler's perspective it was an incredible shot—one of the greatest shots I've played in my life.

On his last shot, Colton hit and rolled to exactly the same place. Now I had a decision to make. Do I try to execute that shot a second time, or do I play an angle raise? We decided to play the angle raise. I was just a little bit tighter than I wanted, a little inside the broom. But with Brett sweeping it from end to end, I made the angle raise for three and we won that game.

I will never forget the feeling in the building. We had just pulled off a Brier playoff win with only three players. We were so pumped.

But we still had to do it twice more. After beating Brendan Bottcher in the semifinal, we faced Kevin Koe of Alberta in the final.

If you go back and look at the video of that game, it's pretty obvious that Brett was under the weather. He was sniffling and his voice was a little bit raspy.

We suspected that he was COVID-positive, but we also knew that if he didn't test, he could play. It was a bit of a moral dilemma. We decided that he would play and that we would do everything we could to keep him away from other people—starting with Jules Owchar who was eighty-two years old and considered to be at high risk.

When I made the last shot to win that game, Geoff and Brett and I embraced and hugged. But we kept that hug a little shorter than normal, and if you look at the pictures, you can see Geoff and me turning our faces away.

A day or two after the Brier, Brett tested positive. I had flown back to Newfoundland with three weeks off before the world championships, and I was still testing negative.

Soon after I got home, my younger daughter, Marissa, tested positive. Then Krista tested positive. Then my parents tested positive.

I was surrounded by COVID. I decided I had to take matters into my own hands. My best bet was to try to get infected as soon as possible so I could get over it in time to head down to Las Vegas for the worlds.

I drove up to our cabin with Marissa and kept the car windows closed the entire way. We stayed the night and I let her sleep in the bed with me. But when we came home, I was still feeling fine and still testing negative.

Finally, five days before the worlds, I was symptomatic. I did a rapid test and it came up positive. The next day I took another one. Still positive.

In order to enter the United States, you needed to present a negative PCR test. I took one just before leaving, and it was clear. The team doctors certified that enough time had passed since the onset of symptoms, and I flew to Las Vegas, arriving a little later than my teammates but in time for the competition.

Meanwhile, the drama with Brett continued.

During the Brier, multiple players from other teams had reached out to me about the next season. That wasn't unusual. During an Olympic year, those conversations start almost immediately after the trials and they continue right through the Brier before things finally start to shake down. Sometimes new teams form even before the Brier. It depends how anxious players are about finding a place to land.

Everyone seemed to know that Brett would be leaving our team. But when I was approached, I had to tell the truth—Brett hadn't told us anything, and I couldn't make any commitments until I knew for sure that he was gone. Well, I didn't know, but I knew. I had heard it from dozens of people by then—players, reporters, officials from Curling Canada. But nothing from the horse's mouth.

The day after the Brier, I started to hear about this team being formed and that team being formed. The player we wanted was E.J. Harnden from Ontario, and now I couldn't wait any longer for Brett to do the right thing. I called him from the airport on the way home and confronted him.

I said, "How come you haven't told me you're leaving the team?"

He said it was true that he was leaving. He told me where he was going. It was the same team I'd heard about back in October.

We had been playing together for almost eleven years. When Brett moved to St. John's, I got him a job, found him an apartment, did everything I could for him. And he didn't have enough courage to tell me the truth—though that's not really the right word, because it doesn't take much courage to say "I'm going to move to Calgary to be with my girlfriend and play with another team."

I was disappointed as a friend and as someone who had a lot of respect for Brett and who hoped he had a lot of respect for me.

Adding E.J. to our team created a new complication—we would be left with only two players from Newfoundland, Mark and me. E.J. is from Northern Ontario and Geoff is from Alberta. Neither of them was born in Newfoundland, which would have been enough to give them residency status. According to Curling Canada rules, three of the four players on a rink had to either live in the province or have been born there.

With E.J. on board, we would be ineligible to represent Newfoundland in the Brier. The only way for us to qualify would be by earning enough points during tour events to claim the spot reserved for the top team in the ranking system. And that would be a huge hurdle.

I contacted Gerry Peckham at Curling Canada, who had seen the way that curling was evolving, with the free movement of players between teams, and was already thinking about possible rule changes.

There was some talk that if you represented a province for multiple Briers, you could get an exemption—for instance, Geoff, who had represented Newfoundland with our team for a long time, would be considered a Newfoundlander for curling purposes. Gerry was also kicking around three or four other possibilities.

Over the course of the three weeks between the Brier and the world championships, we were leaning towards going forward with E.J., but we couldn't commit to him because we weren't sure how it would affect our Brier eligibility.

I shared my behind-the-scenes conversations with Gerry Peckham with Mark and Geoff and Brett.

A half-hour after I talked to Brett, Gerry called me back.

"Brad," he said, "you've got a mole on your team."

"What do you mean?" I asked him.

"I just had two players call me complaining about some of the potential rule changes that you and I discussed. I haven't talked to anybody about them other than you."

Brett had disclosed our private conversation, telling some people what Curling Canada was considering in order to accommodate not only our team but multiple teams that were in the same boat.

I was heartbroken and upset. At that point we were still teammates, we were still going to play together in the world championships, and what happens within a team stays within a team. At least that's the way I've always operated. That trust had been broken.

It felt as though we had been intentionally sabotaged. I can't speak to Brett's intentions, but really there were only two possibilities: Either Brett had simply been gossiping, which wasn't appropriate, or he was trying to squash that potential rule change to prevent us from adding E.J.

The world championships were being held at the Orleans Arena, at the Orleans Hotel and Casino in Las Vegas. We didn't want to stay in a hotel, so we rented what was essentially a two-house compound.

I told the guys that I was going to be staying in one of the houses with E.J., who we brought along as our fifth.

"I don't care who else is in the other house," I said, "but Brett is definitely going to be there."

It was a tense situation. We did our best to keep our relationship cordial on the surface. We had some nice dinners together.

But if there was any discussion about our team's present or future, Brett was not included.

We ended up losing the finals at the worlds. Unfortunately for us, the conditions were not ideal. When they were shaving the ice, one of the edges of their machine dug in and created ridges, which meant that a rock could hit them and fall off. You might experience that as a club curler somewhere, but not at the world-championship level.

We found a way to play through the terrible conditions and we had a chance to win in the final, but Niklas Edin and his Swedish team were much better at handling the poor ice. In Europe, they're not as blessed as we are in Canada, where we almost always play on pristine ice.

And when the tournament was done, that great version of our team was done.

It was a really unfortunate way for it to end. We had been such a strong unit. The four of us had been through a lot together and enjoyed tremendous success.

Brett did reach out later and apologized, which I appreciated. I wish nothing but the best for him going forward. We all have moments in life that we regret and I am no different. There were ways I could have handled the whole situation better, but we have moved past it.

That was a rough stretch for me, from the trials through the Olympics, the Brier and the worlds, all in the middle of an unprecedented global pandemic. No one outside of our team knew about all the other crap we were dealing with.

When you're at the end of a season like that, just about any athlete is going to feel a kind of hangover. You settle back into your home life, and you wonder if you've got it in you to do it all over again. The physical toll, the drama with the team, and now another four-year Olympic cycle looming ahead.

But we had also just won the Olympic trials, won a bronze medal, won the Brier, and played in the final of the worlds. It was going to be really hard for me to shut things down at that point.

I knew I still had a lot left in me.

12

FIGHTING THE GOOD FIGHT

Curlers don't have a union or a players' association like other sports. There was the beginning of one in 2002–3 when the Grand Slams started, but it eventually dissolved. Since then, there have been attempts within the sport to get something going, and I've been involved in a couple of those initiatives, but we have never been able to get it over the hog line.

The reasons why a players' union hasn't taken hold in curling is pretty straightforward: You have to put in a lot of hard work to create such an organization, and then, ultimately, somebody has to run it and there has to be money behind it.

But the unique nature of the sport has also worked against creating a players' union. Curlers are independent contractors. We aren't signed to teams or leagues. We don't get paid a salary. There are no appearance fees for showing up at an event. There is prize money for winning and there are sponsorship deals that we have to seek out ourselves.

But that's it.

It has traditionally been a case of every team, every man or woman, for themselves. And in that type of environment, it's hard to get people to think collectively.

I believe strongly that we really do need some sort of union to represent the players' interests. But very few curlers have been willing to stand up to challenge Curling Canada or the World Curling Federation. What's good for one team doesn't necessarily benefit everybody else.

But there have been a few times when we have stood up for ourselves, like when the eighteen top men's teams boycotted Curling Canada events and moved to the Grand Slam tour in 2001.

Unfortunately, the only way we could make our point about fairness (specifically, about the lack of prize money at the Brier and Curling Canada's refusal to let us wear the logos of our sponsors) was to withhold our services.

The few battles we have fought in the past twenty-five years have mostly taken place behind the scenes. I have been directly involved in a couple of them.

Sponsorship was one issue that pushed me to assume more of an advocacy role. I probably should explain first how that part of the sport works.

Sponsorships make up the financial foundation of every team. That money allows us to travel, to hold training camps, and to hire coaches, physiotherapists, and sports psychologists. We pay for all of that ourselves.

Throughout my career, I have spent the better part of every summer—our off-season—chasing sponsorship dollars for our team. Then during the season it's my job to manage those sponsors by doing everything from photo and commercial shoots to making sure that they get what they need at our events. Most of our sponsors have customers and dealers that come out to events, and it's part of our job to do meet-and-greets and make everybody happy.

As soon as the season ends, and especially at the end of an Olympic quadrennial, I start kicking the tires to find out which sponsors are going to stay with us, and if they're not coming back, to find replacements. Securing new sponsors is the hardest part. It's not like they come looking for us. I have to make cold calls trying to get through to some company's vice-president of marketing, who is generally in Toronto. You have to deal with a lot of gatekeepers along the way, calling back over and over again. Ideally, I can leverage some kind of connection—a friend of a friend—to make inroads. If there's a Newfoundlander involved, that can act as a kind of secret handshake that gets me through the door.

If I can make a pitch face to face, I'm successful 90 percent of the time. The potential sponsor can feel the passion that I have for our team and for the sport. I just have to get in front of them.

Part of that conversation involves telling the sponsor which events the team will be competing in during the season, so they understand how much exposure they're going to get from having their logo on our uniform.

Which brings us to 2017, and one of Curling Canada's major events, the Canada Cup.

At the Brier, which is obviously their biggest event of the year, we aren't allowed to wear sponsor patches on our uniforms, and our sponsors understand that when we make a deal.

But we were told that at the Canada Cup we would be able to wear our normal uniforms with our sponsors' logos. That meant that when we were making our sponsorship deals, we could add the Canada Cup to the list of events where they would get exposure.

Leading up to that first one in 2017, I got a call from Kathy Henderson, who was then the CEO of Curling Canada (you may know her better for a later job, as president and CEO of Hockey Canada), telling me that during the Canada Cup we weren't going to be able to wear the logo of one of our major sponsors, the farm equipment company Kubota.

She explained that they had just signed their own sponsorship deal with New Holland, who were in the same business as Kubota, and that agreement had given New Holland "category exclusivity." No competing brands were allowed.

That was news to me.

Kathy was asking me to go back to Kubota and change the terms of my agreement with them. I flat out said no.

"Our understanding with you about the Canada Cup was that we could wear all of our logos," I told her. "I think you need to go back to New Holland and fix this."

Kathy said that she wasn't prepared to do that.

"Well, if that's the case, we're not going to play the Canada Cup," I told her. "And we're not going to play the Brier. We're also not going to play the international Continental Cup. We're going to boycott all of the Curling Canada events because you're wrong. You're going against the agreement that you had with the players to benefit yourselves."

Just like in 2001, the only real leverage we had as curlers was to walk away. It was the only card I could play.

That was the first time I had ever thrown my weight around. We were the biggest team in curling, the defending Brier champions. And with what happened at the Brier in 2017 in St. John's, Curling Canada knew that our team could sell a lot of tickets for them.

It was also a matter of principle, a hill I was willing to die on. If you're going to impact our sponsors, the people that allow us to play each and every day, I've got to go to bat for them. These companies give us money to go out and compete, to train and to practise. Without them, we wouldn't be who we are. We wouldn't be able to go to the Olympics and take on the rest of the world. I sure wasn't going to let Curling Canada throw our sponsors under the bus.

But I didn't necessarily want to go it alone.

I started talking to Ben Hebert, who played lead on Kevin Koe's team then, and filled him in on the situation. He was not thrilled with what Curling Canada were trying to do and knew that it could have implications for other teams and sponsors in other business categories. If it wasn't New Holland versus Kubota, it could be something else.

Ben and I tried to drum up support from other players. We had a group meeting with a bunch of teams.

Some of them didn't have any issues with category exclusivity because they didn't have any conflicts, so they felt a protest wasn't in their interest.

There were also teams that didn't want to be a part of the challenge because they knew we were going to ruffle feathers. They thought it might somehow adversely affect their government funding, or influence whether or not they were invited to other Curling Canada events.

Most of them just weren't willing to rock the boat.

With no more support on the men's side, we decided to try to get some of the women on board. Manitoba's Chelsea Carey, Alberta's Val Sweeting, and Ontario's Lisa Weagle all stepped up.

They told us that their biggest issue was pay equity: The men were getting significantly more prize money at the Brier than the women were getting at the Scotties. We added that to our list of priorities, along with being able to keep our sponsorship at the Brier and the Scotties, and Ben, Chelsea, Val, and I sat down with Curling Canada. (Lisa subbed for Val in a subsequent meeting.)

That was it. Just the four of us.

The meeting was contentious. We stuck to our positions on a bunch of issues. By the time we had a second meeting, at the Continental Cup in Las Vegas, Curling Canada caved and agreed to allow us to wear our Kubota logos at the Canada Cup that year. They renegotiated their deal with New Holland, which is what should have happened in the first place.

So that was a win—at least for the time being.

But the more important issue was pay equity. That became our cause too. Ben has a daughter and I have two daughters. It just made sense.

In that first meeting, Chelsea did an incredible job of articulating our position and put the leadership of Curling Canada on the ropes. I thought she was super powerful and tipped things in our favour because there was really no arguing the logic of what she said. "You have to give us the same opportunity that the men get," she told them. "You have to put us on a level playing field."

But nonetheless, Curling Canada pushed back hard, maintaining that the Brier brought in more money so the men should get more money. Period.

A few weeks later, much to our surprise, Curling Canada announced that they were going to give the women pay equity at the Scotties. There was no mention of our work behind the scenes, certainly no suggestion that the organization had actually argued against it.

Kathy Henderson took the credit. It was apparently all her idea.

I'm proud that we won that battle, even if we didn't get any acknowledgment for initiating the fight. I just wish more people knew about the incredible job Chelsea, Val, Lisa, and Ben did with me standing up for what was right.

On the sponsorship front, our win turned out to be only temporary. The Canada Cup, and our agreement, only lasted for another couple of years. The event went away for a while and then was replaced by the PointsBet Invitational. Under a new agreement with Curling Canada, they reintroduced category exclusivity. When we renewed deals with our sponsors we had to inform them that their logo wouldn't be included if there was a category conflict. (I really appreciated the fact that Kubota decided to stick with us.)

All of a sudden, I had half a dozen teams telling me they were upset that they couldn't wear their sponsors' logos and asking for my help. Those were some of the same players who wouldn't stand up with me a year earlier when I asked for support because they didn't want to rock the boat.

13

JANUARY 5, 2026

The HearingLife Canadian Open in Saskatoon was my last Grand Slam—and curling fans noticed.

We had a lot of people from all over western Canada come out to watch our team one final time, which was really nice. Before each draw I had people telling me that they had travelled from across the country to see us play. After each game I spent well over an hour talking to fans, signing autographs, getting pictures taken, and sharing memories. It was a cool experience to look back on what I've achieved and how much it mattered to people, hearing them tell me where they were or how old they were when they'd watched some of our biggest games.

I'm not going to lie—I've enjoyed being celebrated a little bit. I feel guilty saying that, but I'm human, and I think most people would react the same way. I haven't allowed myself to enjoy too much of it over the course of my career, not even during this final season. This was the first time this year that I truly started to appreciate the journey I've been on.

Leading up to the Olympic trials, my whole focus had been on getting ready and trying to stay in a competitive zone. I wanted so badly to play well. I've always gone into big events super focused so as not to get distracted by stuff that's going on beyond the rink or outside of the game. Until Saskatoon, that was the way I had been managing this year.

Looking back, I have started to realize that I didn't enjoy myself while competing nearly as much as I should have. But that's on me because I haven't—or couldn't—let myself do so.

Part of me wants to sit back and take in the experience of the final season and part of me is still thinking that I need to concentrate on every game in order to play as well as I can. Over the last month, especially, it has been an internal battle.

I definitely want to enjoy what is coming up with my last Brier, since it's going to be in St. John's. And I also want to play well there. I don't want to finish my career with a whimper. I want to go out and give our team a chance to win even if in the end we don't win it all. Having played for as long as I have, I know what I need to do to be successful. I have always relied on that focus and that intensity.

Trying to find a balance of enjoying the moment while focusing on what I have to do on the ice has been a real challenge, and I'm not sure which way I'm going to go. I definitely want to take it all in, but I also know that I have to go through my normal process to be ready for each and every game.

In Saskatoon, I allowed myself to appreciate the moment and somehow still played really well.

Unfortunately, we had a rough quarterfinal game against John Shuster of the U.S., where he was very good and we wound up on the wrong side of it. But at the end of the day, it was both our best event of the season and the one that I enjoyed the most.

During the event in Saskatoon, the guys and I spent some time reminiscing about past Grand Slams and talking about how much the tour has changed since we started.

Back in 2001, when we were starting out, there was a big fracture in the Canadian curling world. Eighteen of the best men's teams broke off to play on what was then the new Grand Slam tour while boycotting the Brier, because none of the money there flowed through to the players (there wasn't even any prize money) and because teams couldn't feature their own sponsors on their uniforms. The Brier had become a huge event where they were filling NHL rinks like the Northlands Coliseum in Edmonton and the Saddledome in Calgary for the whole week, with two hundred thousand tickets sold, and all that money went to Curling Canada. Other than having their basic expenses covered, the curlers didn't get a dime. If you decided to bring your family along, you could win the Brier and still come home actually losing money.

When the players said that they wanted a share of that revenue, plus a chance to showcase their sponsors, Curling Canada said no. That's when the split happened. Those teams separated, formed the Grand Slam, and boycotted the Curling Canada events, including the Brier. As a player and as a team, you had to choose which side you were on.

Our team was in a unique place then because we were just coming out of juniors. Since we weren't one of the best eighteen teams in the country, we weren't asked to join the group that was boycotting the Brier. But when one of those teams couldn't make a Slam and they needed someone to fill in, we were always the first called. We were young, and the organizers wanted to support our development.

Plus, we hadn't taken sides during the split. Guys like Randy Ferbey, Russ Howard, and John Morris had turned the Slammers down. Because we were never asked, we didn't have to say yes or no, so there was no bad blood with the organizers.

During those years we'd play a couple of Slams a season and still be eligible to play in the Brier representing Newfoundland and Labrador. We had the best of both worlds.

I remember the excitement when the Slams started. They were brand-new top-of-the-line events played in big arenas around the country and with great TV coverage. Being part of that, even if it was only a couple of times a year, played a huge role in our development as a team. We were fresh out of juniors and now we were playing in front of big crowds on arena ice in similar conditions to what you'd find at a Brier or world championship. It helped prepare us for what was to come.

In 2004 the Slammers made a deal with Curling Canada that included prize money at the Brier for the first time (but they still didn't allow sponsor logos on the uniforms). By then we were good enough to qualify for the tour.

We had a ton of success in Grand Slams through the years and enjoyed playing in some great events.

But looking back, I think that the split in the curling community prevented the series from reaching its full potential. By 2012, they were in real trouble. That's when Rogers Communications stepped in and bought the series.

Rogers did a great job at the start. As players, we could see the growth of the Slams. The events started selling out and Rogers expanded the series from four to seven events. And then it went from seven back to five, but we were still seeing a lot of sellouts.

At the end of the 2024 season, Nic Sulsky of The Curling Group bought the Grand Slams from Rogers and, as I mentioned earlier, some dramatic changes have taken place during the past year. I hope they will be successful.

Over the course of my career, I've seen the Grand Slams go from being really successful to being on the brink of collapse to undergoing crazy change. I'm uncertain how it's going to end up. The world is a different place than it was in 2001. People's attention spans are even shorter. The demographic that has loyally supported our sport over the years is much older now.

With the Rock League, Nic and his team are trying to do something so different from what we've done in the past in the hope of attracting a younger audience. If he's right, we will see huge growth in the sport. If he's wrong, it could set it back.

That change was definitely a factor in my decision to retire. It is an uncertain time. If I had committed to four more years, I would have had no idea what the sport was going to look like at the end of that time, or what position the curlers were going to be in. I think watching from the outside, at my age, at this stage of my career, is fine by me.

Heading into Saskatoon, we knew that we were unlikely to qualify for the Players' Championship in January. We weren't one of the top twelve teams in the world rankings.

That left me facing one of the quietest stretches I've had since I began curling competitively. We will probably look for a small event just to keep sharp, but otherwise we have nothing scheduled until the Brier begins.

I know what's coming in St. John's. My emotions are going to be amped up so much more than they were in Saskatoon, and the attention is going be infinitely greater. I'm bracing for the experience to be really intense. I don't know how I'll handle it, and that uncertainty leads to a lot of anxiety. But everybody around me has been encouraging me to enjoy it as much as I can.

That's what I want to do. I'm just not sure I'll be able to.

I still feel that I will be selling myself short if I don't go out and give the same kind of commitment and preparation that I've done in the past. Even if that means not smelling as many roses as I should along the way, I think, at the end of the day, I will be happier.

The good news is that physically, I'm in a great place right now. I wish I had felt like this five or six years ago.

I'm proud that I did a really good job getting my body back to where it should be. I was so concerned that by the time we got to St. John's I was going to be in such poor physical shape, with my hip and back issues, that I wouldn't be able to play my best. But that's not an excuse I'm going to have now. I feel strong, I feel healthy, I'm not playing with the pain that I have been dealing with for such a long time, so that's exciting.

When I've played in big events over the past ten years, it really was like curling rehab. This time around—assuming my body holds up for another month—I'm going to enjoy knowing that I shouldn't be facing the limitations that I've dealt with in the last few Briers.

At the end of the day, I've been lucky enough to play well even when I had those aches and pains. I won Briers when I wasn't close to 100 percent.

And on the flip side, I know that just because I'm feeling great this time doesn't mean that I'll play great.

Let's see what happens in St. John's.

14

BACK-TO-BACK

The 2023 Brier in London, Ontario, was a fun one. I have always liked that city and the people there have always treated us very well. Heading into the tournament as defending champions, I was feeling comfortable about how our team had been performing. We were finishing up our first full season with E.J. after the split with Brett, and that created some extra excitement within the group.

In the end, it wasn't the best Brier we ever played—not even close—but it went smoothly. We were solid enough to finish the round robin 10–1. I remember Geoff being especially good for us that week.

In our first playoff game, we went up against Mike McEwen and won that pretty easily. That put us in with Matt Dunstone in the Page 1-2 game, which meant E.J. was going to have to play his brother Ryan, who was the lead on Matt's team.

It was, understandably, a difficult game for E.J., so we did our best to support him as much as we could. We squeaked through 5–4, which put us into the final.

Matt was matched up against Brendan Bottcher in the semis, which meant that our opponent would either be Brendan's team, which now had Brett Gallant playing with them—that would have been a bit of a tough situation for us, given the sour way things ended with Brett the year before—or Team Dunstone again, which would have been another nightmare for the Harnden family.

In the end, Matt beat Brendan, setting up Harnden versus Harnden one more time. I can only imagine the stress that E.J. and Ryan were going through playing against each other in the Brier final. And their poor parents—who do you cheer for? In the end you know that one of your children is going to be excited beyond belief and the other one is going to be devastated. (I speak from personal experience. A couple of years ago, I watched Marissa play against Hayley in a U-16 event. It was agonizing.)

We played a very good game in the final. In the eighth end, we scored three to go up by three. And then in the ninth, we forced Team Dunstone to take two, which was all that we were trying to do. That left us one up with the hammer coming home.

In that last end, we were in a good position with skip rocks to come. And then Matt got fortunate with his final throw. It wasn't exactly the way he had planned to make the shot, but somehow after the dust settled, he managed to roll into an area where they were lying two and I didn't have anything available to hit. Matt inadvertently left me with the hardest shot that I could have had in that situation.

I had assumed he was going to make the shot he was trying to make, so I planned a completely different scenario in my head, one where I would be playing a relatively straightforward quiet-weight hit with my last rock to win the Brier.

Instead, I was faced with a draw to the four-foot down a path that we hadn't played since much earlier in the game, and I also had to put the shot through a tight gap between two rocks.

What added to the pressure was that I had to make it with Matt lying two—meaning that if I missed, we would lose. Unlike my last shot at the 2018 Brier, there was no extra-end safety net.

As soon as I let the rock go, I knew it wasn't my best throw. And because we didn't know the path it would take, I wasn't 100 percent certain that, even if I executed well, it was going to end up in the right line or have the right distance.

E.J. and Geoff were off and on it, and if the sweepers do that it's usually a pretty good sign that you're close. I was watching the line, and it seemed to be exactly where we wanted the shot to be.

As the rock approached the hog line, I thought, *Hopefully this thing tracks like it should, because it looks like it's in pretty good shape.* And then shortly after it crossed the line, I heard E.J. say, "Back four."

Back four was fine. It was all we needed. But if he had misjudged it, even by a foot or two, there would still have been a chance that the shot could wind up going a little bit too far.

As the rock approached the rings, I could see Mark getting amped up. He knew before I did that we had made it. As it slid over the top of the twelve-foot he started to celebrate.

The rock stopped back button. We had won another Brier.

I think I was more relieved than excited because so much had been at stake and I knew that I hadn't thrown the rock as well as I could have.

After the celebration, our thoughts turned to E.J. and his family. He was so pumped to win, but I know it had to be tough for the Harndens. Ryan is a first-class guy and handled everything extremely well. We all had a good time celebrating afterwards. But man oh man, I just can't imagine what E.J. and Ryan had to go through during that game.

That win was particularly satisfying for me because it came after Brett had left the team the year before. I wanted to prove to everyone that we were still the best team in curling without him, and I wanted to show him that the way he had handled his departure wasn't the right one. Winning a Brier is always great, but for Geoff, Mark, and me, winning that one came with extra satisfaction.

But our biggest excitement was for E.J. and our new coach, Caleb Flaxey, curling veterans whose only Brier win had come with Brad Jacobs a decade before. The rest of us were pretty spoiled because of the success we had enjoyed over the past six years. To see their excitement and how pumped they were—that was the best part of all.

♣

A year later, the Brier was back in Regina, a place where we'd had a ton of success. We stayed at the same hotel where we stayed when we won in 2018. We were back in the same rink, the same dressing room. All those memories created a lot of good vibes for us the minute we arrived at the Brandt Centre.

We were playing well in 2024, maybe not at our absolute peak but good enough to leave us feeling confident about our chances of winning a third Brier in a row.

A lot of people probably remember that tournament because of an incident that happened in our very first game of the round robin against Matthew Manuel's team from Nova Scotia.

A guy and a girl were sitting in the first row of the crowd, leaning over the boards. Normally you get the odd person at the rink who is really excited to be down close to the players. But this guy was at a whole different level. He decided he was going to involve himself in the game and he started heckling us—especially Mark, who he was really picking on. It was stupid juvenile stuff: "You suck," "You're fat." He was trying to get in our heads and get us off our game. It turned out that he was a buddy of one of the guys on the Nova Scotia rink, and needless to say he'd had a few too many drinks. I've dealt with hecklers before, but none had ever been as persistent as this guy.

We went into that game as big favourites, but it turned out to be really tight.

In the ninth end, we were up 5–4 with the hammer. I was in the hack getting ready to play a runback. In situations like that, I'm so focused on the shot that I'm oblivious to anything that is going on around me.

E.J. was standing right next to me. All of a sudden I heard him telling the guy in the crowd to shut the fuck up, and my concentration broke.

I had been so zoned in on the shot that I didn't hear what the guy had been saying to me. But E.J. heard, and he was concerned that it was going to distract me.

The guy came back at E.J., E.J. went back at him, and it became a bit of a scene.

Eventually it got to a point where we had to get the heckler out of there. I called a time out, went to an official, and asked to have the guy and his girlfriend removed.

It took five or ten minutes to resolve things, which is a long time in between shots in the world of curling.

I settled back in the hack and ended up making the shot. We scored two to pull ahead 7–4, and Matthew Manuel shook to end the game.

This may sound strange considering that it was just a round-robin game against Nova Scotia in the very early stages of a Brier, but all things considered, that was one of the shots I'm most proud of in my career. All of the mental training we do in order to compete doesn't always work, but in that case it really paid off.

There was an infamous incident during the 2004 Brier final when a guy kept heckling the Ferbey Four, who were going for their fourth consecutive win. Marcel Rocque, who played lead for Randy, confronted the guy the same way that E.J. did. But it rattled the team, they lost their composure, and it might have contributed to them losing the Brier that year.

Instead of us falling apart, the incident with the heckler galvanized us that week. E.J. took a little bit of heat from folks for going after the guy, but at the end of the day he was sticking up for me and sticking up for his teammates.

We only lost a couple of times in the round robin, to Jamie Koe from the Territories (just like we did in 2017) and to Mike McEwen.

In the first playoff game, we beat Reid Carruthers, which put us in against Brendan Bottcher's rink, including Brett.

It wasn't particularly dramatic. We had the hammer to start, got two right away, and controlled the rest of the game, winning 7–3.

We had to wait for the winner of the semifinal between Bottcher and Mike to find out who our opponents would be in the final. McEwen had one of his "Magic Mike" games and the whole team played great, curling 93 percent on their way to the win. As I watched that match I was thinking, *If they play like that against us, we're going to have a hard time.*

In the final, we got two early to go ahead, and then I made a really nice double in the fourth end to score three and put us up 5–1. We forced Team McEwen to take a single in the fifth end and went into the break up three with the hammer.

If you look at the analytics, we had at least a 95 percent chance of winning at that point. And then we came out in the sixth end and had one of the worst ends I've been part of in my career. We missed the first six shots. By the time I got in the hack it looked like we might give up a steal of three or four.

On my last rock, I made a really tough shot to hold them to a steal of two. Most average curling fans might have thought that I'd messed up, because of the score. But the truth is, it was the only shot that I had and it kept us in the lead, up 5–4 with the hammer, so still in a really good position.

I will always remember that sixth end. It's not very often that a shot giving up a steal of two is the biggest one you're going to throw in a Brier. But people who really know the sport understand just how important it was.

That said, heading into the seventh end, the momentum was definitely on Mike's side.

We had a brief team meeting but there really wasn't much to be said. Just standard stuff: "Let's go, we're still in good shape."

And then we came back in the seventh and played an end that was almost as bad, immediately getting ourselves back into trouble.

On my first shot of the end, I made a runback that at least blew up what was happening in the four-foot and put us in a position where we were going to have a shot to score, no matter what Mike did with his last rock.

Mike played a draw, trying to apply as much pressure as he could. Unfortunately for him, the shot didn't curl quite as much as he had hoped. He left me an opening to hit a piece of the rock and make a double. It was a very difficult shot—one that I would probably miss more often than I would make. But one of the luxuries of having E.J. on our team was knowing that he was the best and most powerful sweeper in the world. If I put it on the right line, E.J. could hold it there.

I threw the stone exactly the way I wanted to. As soon as I let go, E.J. got on it. He swept it the whole way down. We ended up hitting an inch of their rock, ricocheting into another one, and scoring two.

I remember looking up into the crowd and seeing the Gushue Girls there—the six women from Gander who have travelled all over the place to watch us play. (Remember, we were playing against Team Saskatchewan in Regina. We were not the favourites in that building—which is abnormal for us when we play just about anywhere in Canada.)

I looked up at the Girls and my parents, who were sitting near them, and gave them the biggest fist pump that I could manage. I was really trying to get our team fired up after playing two of the worst ends that we had ever played together.

We were up three without the hammer—so the game still wasn't a foregone conclusion, but we were at least in a much better position to win.

As it turned out, that seventh end turned the tide. We forced Team McEwen to take one in the eighth, and in the ninth we scored two. Then they shook.

That was my sixth Brier title.

When I think back now, winning that first one in 2017 was nice because I finally got what I had craved since I was a kid, and of course I got to do it at home.

Winning the second one proved that the first one wasn't a fluke.

The third put us in a pretty rarefied place.

For me, the fourth Brier was really important because I joined a select group with Kevin Martin, Kevin Koe, Ernie Richardson, and Randy Ferbey, the only other guys who won four championships as skips. As far as I'm concerned, those guys are the curling Mount Rushmore.

Up until that point, nobody had won more than four Briers as a skip. Winning my fifth in 2023 meant that I was all alone.

Randy Ferbey was the only player who had won six Briers in total—four as a skip and two as a third. By winning the sixth one in 2024, Mark, Geoff, and I joined him. No player has won more than Randy, Mark, Geoff, and I have.

And in 2026, we were chasing number seven.

Whenever I get interviewed before the Brier, my stock answer is that those numbers don't mean much to me. It's all about the here and now.

But the truth is, making history is what motivates me.

It's not something that you necessarily think about in the moments after you win a final. You're still wrapped up in the intensity of the game and the excitement of winning that particular championship.

But later in the night or the next morning, when you're sitting in the airport getting ready to fly home, or in the days and weeks that follow, you start thinking about those numbers—four and five and six—and you can't help thinking, *Damn, this is pretty cool.*

15

TOBY

Outside of my parents, my sister, my wife, and my kids, no one has been a bigger influence on my life than Toby McDonald.

Toby was part of the rink skipped by Jack MacDuff that won Newfoundland's first Brier, in 1976, well before I was born. They were crazy underdogs who came out of nowhere and had a magical week. It's a pretty incredible story.

When they came home, they were heroes.

That's one of the reasons I felt that he understood better than anyone else some of the challenges that I faced as a successful curler from Newfoundland.

When I was growing up and hanging around the club, I remember Toby having a kind of aura about him. Jack wasn't living in the province by then and you'd only see the other guys from that team, Doug Hudson and Ken Templeton, occasionally. But Toby was still active at the club as a competitive curler.

I was a teenager the first time I got to play against him, and I remember thinking, *I'm playing a Brier champion.* I knew he was really good and really smart. And he was always very kind to me.

When he agreed to coach our team, I was shocked. Toby was a

busy guy, a successful lawyer with his own firm in St. John's. How do you take on coaching some juniors when you've got that much going on?

We needed him to travel with us to a lot of our events, including our first Grand Slams and international competitions. In 2005, leading into the Olympic trials, Curling Canada wanted us to get some international experience, so they paid for our flights to two back-to-back events in Norway. One was an under-25 competition that ended up being a big drunk for all the other teams, though we took it fairly seriously, and the other was a World Curling Tour event with a lot of the top European teams.

We were overseas for just under two weeks, and Toby agreed to go with us on his own dime.

I think anybody who has been to Norway knows it's a pretty expensive place, but in those days, we weren't aware of that. Our first day there we had dinner at the hotel restaurant, and a club sandwich and fries cost forty-five dollars Canadian. We were trying to pinch pennies, all living in the same room, so we definitely weren't going to be eating club sandwiches every day. (Toby was on the Atkins diet at the time—he just ate bacon all day.)

We found a gas station down the road from the hotel that sold taquitos for a couple of bucks each, which was a price we could actually afford. For the whole two weeks we were in Europe, that's all we ate, other than the free breakfasts at the hotel.

And as for Toby's compensation, we certainly didn't pay very well—as in, we didn't pay at all. We didn't have the income or the resources in those days. His was purely a volunteer role.

But Toby still agreed to take the time away from his job and his family (he had two kids slightly younger than I was at the time) to help us.

I could tell right from the start that Toby had a different approach from any coach I had encountered before or have encountered since.

Curling coaches do a lot of different things. They can help you on the ice with how you throw the rock and otherwise hone your skills. They can improve how a team communicates. They can provide strategic advice, helping you to make the right decisions on certain shots.

The really good coaches, in addition to all that, work behind the scenes to make your team better off the ice. That part is all about getting to know each other and understanding what works in pressure moments and what doesn't. Toby understood the human side of curling in a way that in those days I did not. He knew how to get the most out of people, how to develop empathy, how to help teammates perform.

Toby's approach was never super technical. From a curling standpoint, he was old school—get that rock down to the spot and it doesn't really matter how you get it there. That was the polar opposite of me. I always wanted to be technically strong. But he could connect with me on a personal level too. He was a great sounding board as well as a bit of a psychologist. Toby was someone who could help me work through my thoughts. In some ways he was as much a life coach as a curling coach.

He could do all of that while at the same time being an incredible person.

There were a couple of conversations I had with Toby that quite literally changed my life.

The first was when I was getting ready to propose to Krista. Toby knew her and loved her. When I started talking to him about getting married, he was 100 percent on board.

"This is the right time for you to do it, absolutely," he said to me.

That's how close our relationship was. I went to him for that kind of personal advice—how to propose, when to do it. It was about so much more than just curling. I had conversations with him when Krista and I were thinking about having kids, asking him what it was going to be like to be a parent.

When I was facing a dilemma over whether there was a way to continue to curl at a high level and still be a good father and run a business, Toby was there to advise me.

Oftentimes he'd just listen, and still I would leave a conversation or a dinner with Toby feeling better than when we started. Krista could always see the change in me. When Toby and I would go out and have a bite to eat or meet at his office, I'd walk away from it feeling more confident about a decision that I had looming or the situation I was in, or just about life in general.

Toby was also my lawyer, so he was actively involved when I was opening businesses or buying real estate. We had so many things in common—curling, fatherhood, being business owners, and having some notoriety in Newfoundland.

Our second big conversation came in 2011, when I was ready to quit the game and Toby talked me out of it—but not before telling me hard truths about how I had to improve as a skip and as a leader.

In the moment, I was pissed because he had called me out. Part of me still believed it was everybody else's fault that our team wasn't having as much success as we should. But the reality was that I was the one to blame, because I wasn't leading the team as well as I should have. I wasn't creating a good environment for the players around me because I was too much of a hard-ass.

Here I was thinking, *Why isn't everybody willing to do what I'm doing? Why can't they go out and throw 150 rocks a day? Why can't they spend hours in the gym? Why is their life not revolving around the sport the way mine does?*

Toby was the one who told me, flat out, that the way I treated my teammates had to change. It was not what I wanted to hear, but it was what I needed to hear.

In 2012 we brought in Adam Casey and Geoff Walker, and then Brett Gallant came in the following year. By the time Mark Nichols came back after his four years away, I was a much different player, and a much more patient skip and leader than the guy he used to play with.

And that's a big reason why we started down the road that eventually led to six Briers and another trip to the Olympics.

Toby was our formal coach for only a short time. He was with us for the 2004–5 and 2005–6 seasons, which included the Turin Olympics. Then he became too busy with his law firm and stepped away.

He came back to coach our team with Ryan Fry, Geoff Walker, and Adam Casey at the Brier in 2012.

We didn't have a good competition, finishing 5–6, and I played especially poorly, probably the worst Brier of my career.

Very rarely did Toby give me direct advice. But when he did, I definitely listened.

At the end of that Brier, Toby came to me and said, "Brad, I love what you're doing with Geoff and Adam, but you need to move on from Ryan. You're two different people out there. And Ryan is bringing out the worst in you."

Ryan was playing incredibly well then. He was as good as anyone at that Brier. But we let him go two weeks later and everybody in the curling world was shocked—they thought I had just cut the best player on our team.

Toby played a big role in the development of the team after that. We had that great run with Geoff and Brett and Adam coming back. He became especially good friends with Geoff and really took him under his wing.

Toby and I liked to get together at our favourite restaurant in St. John's, Basho. He was in there so often that they named a dish after him, the Toby Plate, which is a big selection of sushi and is still on the menu.

He'd allow me the space to share what I needed to share and he'd provide advice. But mostly he was a friend who would listen and who

I could trust. My inner circle is really small. There aren't many people I trust that way. Toby was right at the centre of that circle.

He was heavily involved in the decision to move on from E.J. Harnden in 2024 and bring in Brendan Bottcher. That was also around the time when Toby started to get really sick. I remember him asking me for Brendan's phone number. "I just want to have a chat with him," he said. Brendan would be joining us mid-season, and Toby wanted to get a feel for him as a person, and to give Brendan an idea of how we operated and what he could do to make me, and make Mark, better players.

That was about a month before Toby passed. Thinking back, I realize how incredible it was that he was willing to do that for us given how sick he was. That's how much he cared. It felt like he was keeping his arms around the team, and around me.

We had one last dinner at Basho just before Christmas in 2024.

Soon after that, Toby went into the hospital. We had been on the road at an event in Guelph, Ontario, so I wasn't even aware of it. When I got back home, I went to the rink to practise, and Jeff Thomas, who's been a coach of ours for a long time, told me that Toby had entered palliative care. I had no idea his cancer had worsened so fast. Then his business partner called: "Toby has taken a turn," she said. "If you want to come see him, come now."

I got off the ice right away.

By the time I got to the hospice, Toby could no longer communicate. His wife, Noreen, left me alone in the room with him, and I remember thinking that I should have done a better job of letting him know how much he meant to me. I should have thanked him more. I wish I had shared how much I appreciated everything he had done for me, how grateful I was. I think he deserved to be told.

It's a shame that we didn't recognize him as much as we should have when he was still with us.

The night before Toby's funeral, the five of us from the 2006 Olympics went out for dinner. Mark and Russ and Mike and Jamie and I started telling Toby stories and talking about the private conversations he'd had with us.

It was amazing how all of those conversations had a common thread. Individually and as a team, Toby was always working to make us better. At the Olympics, we were overwhelmed by the experience and we struggled at first before righting the ship and winning the gold medal.

I realize now that Toby had a bigger role in our winning than I gave him credit for at the time. He kept us grounded and focused. He was such a huge part of our success.

♣

The time of Toby's passing coincided with the start of talk around the pro league. I was struggling with my performance on the ice and really starting to wonder if it was time for me to retire.

And then suddenly Toby was gone and I was left to deal with all that without the one person who I trusted most to help me. The second half of that season was pretty challenging.

But I did come away having learned an important lesson. Now, I try to tell people how grateful I am for them. I'm still not good at it, but I am aware and I am working on it.

That's a positive, I guess, but I wish I'd done it more for Toby. That's my biggest regret.

16

FEBRUARY 23, 2026

There were two and a half months between our last game at the Olympic trials and our first game at an event we just played in Saskatchewan. That's one of the longest breaks I've ever had during a curling season since I was a teenager. I had no idea how I was going to respond to that much time off. The truth is, I really enjoyed it.

We got the team together for a training camp in Edmonton for a few days in January (we couldn't get ice time in St. John's, so Mark and I had to make the trip west) and then we played in the Curling Stadium Martensville International, just outside Saskatoon, to shake off some of the rust.

If you'd asked me any time in the last few years to go and play a smaller bonspiel in Saskatchewan at a four-sheet curling club, I would've said, "Oh my God, are you serious?"

After the Olympic trials in November, I didn't have a whole lot of desire to compete. I think the other guys on the team felt the same way. But by that point in the new year I was excited just to get back on the ice.

We had a lot of fun in Martensville. The organizers sold the place out, the ice was great, and it was good to get the guys sweeping, calling the line, and doing all the things that we're going to be doing next week at the Brier in St. John's.

In Martensville there were ten teams in two pools of five, so we played four round-robin games. Some good rinks were there—Mike McEwen, Jordon McDonald of Manitoba (who ended up beating Mike's team in the final), Rylan Kleiter of Saskatchewan, plus three American teams who came up to get ready for their national championship.

We went undefeated in the round robin and then unfortunately lost the semifinal to Jordon's team in an extra end.

Our games overall were a little bit of shit and honey. I was feeling pretty good physically. In the round robin, Brendan was playing as well as I've ever seen him play, and Geoff was really strong. Mark was kind of up and down. And then we played the semifinal and Brendan went from being the best player in the building to having the worst game I've ever seen him play with us.

We were all over the place, but at the moment I like how we're throwing the rock. Heading into the Brier, I think we're going to be peaking at the right time.

We are about to begin a pre-Brier camp here in St. John's. The guys are flying in tomorrow if the snow allows (what a crazy winter we've had here). We'll have four days of training at the St. John's Curling Club. That should be enough for a final tune-up and to get us throwing our paths and trajectories the way we want.

Other than the one game in Saskatchewan, Brendan looks like he's playing well, which is part of what we've missed for the last year and a half. We wanted the Brendan who went to three Brier finals in a row between 2018 and 2020, but I think the last couple of years of inconsistency have really taken their toll on his confidence. Now he seems to be getting that back, which is exciting because at his best Brendan is one of the top players in the world.

It's no surprise that the guys have been planning for what they'll do after my retirement at the end of the season.

It's always a wild time just after the Brier finishes. That's when you find out which teams are sticking together and who is going where. It can be like a big game of musical chairs. It would make for a really good Netflix special. Imagine being in those backrooms and putting a camera on every single top player around the country, listening to some of the conversations around putting teams together and trying to decide what is true and when someone is feeding you a line. I know I'd watch it.

When you're at the top of the food chain, it's a lot easier to get the players you want. That's where I was at the end of the last couple of quadrennials. Teams and free-agent players would wait to see what I was doing before they made a move. But when you're the skip of a third- or fourth-ranked team, you feel pretty vulnerable at times because even though you want to attract certain guys to play with, you might not be their first choice. You have to wait and see how how things that you have no control over shake out.

There are several considerations in play when teams break up or reconfigure. Obviously, everyone wants to be part of a team that's going to compete at a high level. Ideally, they want to be with guys who they get along with too. Location also matters—logistically, it's easier living in some parts of the country than in others. Joining a team that you know is going to get into the Grand Slams is also a big plus.

After the quality of the people, one of the most important considerations is sponsorship money. If a team is bringing in enough money that a player knows his costs for the year are going to be completely paid for before you start, that's a huge selling point.

When Brendan asked me for advice about assembling a team, I told him, "Don't go out and find someone that's accomplished everything and is thirty-five years old. They're probably on the downward side of their career trajectory. Go out and get the best young players you can find." (It was a lot like the advice Toby gave me years ago.)

Brendan figured it out and got things done early. He's going to be skipping a new team that includes Geoff as well as Tanner and Jake Horgan, who played with John Epping this year. They'll announce that right after the Brier.

If I was going to continue to curl and was looking for players, Tanner and Jake would be near the top of my list. I've been super impressed with how they've played and how they've improved over the last couple of years. They're young guys that are only going to get better.

And as for Mark's plans?

Well, that's still a bit of a mystery.

We've all tried to talk to him about it, but so far he's been noncommittal. He doesn't know what he wants to do. He's said to me that if he does play, he probably wants to skip a team. Mark has skipped in mixed doubles before and even won the Canadian mixed curling championship in 2005. But he's had very limited experience skipping at the men's level.

If he decides to play, that's the route he's going to go, but if he doesn't move soon, he won't have a lot of options to pick from.

Being based in Newfoundland makes things a lot more

challenging. Residency isn't as much of an issue as it once was, because teams can focus on getting to the Brier through the wild-card and points routes instead of trying to be eligible by winning their home province. For instance, Brendan and Geoff are based in Edmonton and Tanner and Jake are in Ontario. You might see one of the Ontario guys move west, but their goal is to put together the best possible team and then figure everything else out afterwards. I think that's the right approach.

But in Mark's case, if he does decide to put together a team, he could be the lone Newfoundlander on the squad, because I don't believe there would be options for him here in terms of players from here.

If he recruits guys from other parts of Canada, you're not going to have three guys travelling to Newfoundland every weekend to train. Among other things, that means it could be lonely for him. He could wind up flying to events by himself and practising by himself a lot of the time. I don't believe there's anybody else here at a level where they could even be a buddy for him to practise with. That's a challenge that Mark is going to have to face, and I'm sure it's factoring into his decision.

But that's all speculation. So far Mark really hasn't shared a whole lot and he hasn't sought my advice. I've asked a couple of times and gotten crickets, so I've just let it go. I don't think he's talked to Brendan or Geoff or our coach Jeff. It's a bit of a mystery at this point, and to be honest, it feels a little odd.

But maybe Mark just wants to make that decision on his own, and if that's the case, I have to respect it. He's obviously not ready to talk, but if he doesn't move soon, the decision is going to be made for him by everybody else.

The one thing that could be holding him up is waiting to find out what the Jacobs team is going to do. If Marc Kennedy decides to call it a day, that would open up an opportunity that would affect the free-agent market. And there's a chance another member of the team, Ben Hebert, might pack it in too. But the rumour that was going around before the Olympics was that Ben was going to play one more year because he wants to finish with a Brier win at home in Saskatchewan, since the 2027 tournament is in Saskatoon.

My guess is that Ben and Marc, being good buddies, are probably going to go out at the same time. Unless something changes in the next few days, I think most of the other teams have probably also made that assumption and moved on with their decisions.

Speaking of Marc Kennedy, the other thing that I've been doing during this time off is watching the Olympics from Italy—more than I would normally.

The last couple of times that I didn't make it to the Games, I didn't watch them at all. I was too bitter, too sour, and too immature to enjoy them.

But I guess I've grown up a bit. I really enjoyed watching the Olympics this time. It's been interesting seeing some of the challenges that the teams faced that felt so familiar to me. I remember in Beijing, it felt like every shot was an uphill battle for us. It looked that way at times for Rachel Homan and Bruce Mouat of Great Britain, who are the two top teams in the world. Both of them had to fight through to get to the playoffs, which is what we did in Beijing.

The Olympics are such a different beast. People are more amped up, they're more nervous, everything is a little harder. Everything seems a bit more pristine and unfamiliar when you're out there on the ice.

Bruce is the best player in the world—and I don't say that

lightly, because that was me for ten years, but I certainly feel that he has eclipsed me now.

But he had a hard time finding his groove at the Olympics.

Bruce made that great runback triple against Switzerland in the semifinal that is one of the best shots you'll ever see. But he wasn't at his best in the final, whereas Jacobs and his team played really well to win the gold medal. Congratulations to them.

Of course, a lot of people have been asking me what I thought about the Marc Kennedy "double touch" incident against Sweden and the reaction afterwards.

There were a whole lot of wrongs there. When you look at Marc's throw where it all started, there were technically two violations. One, he double-touched the granite, which in fact is something widely accepted in the world of curling—so widely accepted that none of us who were playing in Martensville while the Olympics were going on actually knew it was against the rules.

I've never seen it called as a violation, and I've never seen anybody approach another player on it.

Everybody knows that that's how Marc throws a rock, so nobody really gave it a second thought. As long as it's done before the hog line, it shouldn't be an issue.

But even if you happen to go over the hog line, if it's just by an inch or two, curlers assume you're not trying to do that deliberately. It's a gentleman's game. And the reality is, the impact 140 feet down the ice is negligible.

Marc was over the hog line when he double-touched, which was technically the second violation.

The problem I had with the whole thing was with the way the Swedish team approached it. Judging from their interviews afterwards, it sure seemed premeditated, which is not in the spirit of our sport. If it was an issue for them, they could have addressed it well before the game and not embarrassed the Canadian team the way they did.

I assume they handled it the way they did in an effort to put Marc off his game. That seems to have been the intent, especially given that the Swedish team didn't complain about it until the third end. That was so inappropriate. It caused a black eye for the sport over something that's not really of any consequence.

But none of that would have become much of a story if Marc didn't react the way he did. If he had brushed it off and walked away, it would have been forgotten. Unfortunately, because of the way he responded with some strong language, it became a worldwide news story and forced the World Curling Federation to enforce a rule that has never, ever been enforced.

In my opinion, it was a non-issue.

There was plenty of blame to go around. There were wrongs on the Swedish side, on the Canadian side with Marc's reaction, and certainly in how the World Curling Federation handled it, bringing in officials to monitor games.

It's going to be interesting to see how the rule is called at the world championships in April.

Now we have entered the home stretch before the Brier. There is just about a week to go before things kick off in St. John's.

Our team has done some things to prepare for the week, but our planning has been nowhere near as detailed as it was in 2017. At this point, at least from my standpoint, I think the challenge is going to be mostly emotional.

I don't feel the pressure and the stress to perform the way I did the last time. Obviously I still want to win and I want to play well. But my biggest concern right now is whether I'm going to wind up crying every single day.

When the home crowd gives me a standing ovation, I'm probably going to melt. That's my biggest stress and worry. I don't want to do that. I want to be able to stay focused and go through the normal routine that I would if I were playing in a Brier anywhere else.

For the Brier week we have rented a house not too far from the Mary Brown's Centre. That should alleviate a lot of the distraction that we had when we stayed at a hotel during the Brier in 2017 and during the St. John's Slam last year. There were fans waiting outside my door and waiting for us when we got off the hotel elevator and as we were walking over to the rink. It felt like people were on top of us all the time.

I understand that the fans are emotional and that they have high expectations of us. I can't tell you how many times since I announced my retirement that I've had people come up to me crying because I was stepping away and begging me not to retire. It's been a little bit wild. Avoiding those types of situations as much as possible over the next two weeks is going to be important for us.

Having the house to ourselves will give us some privacy and allow us to cook our own meals and stay away from the restaurant scene. At the rink, Curling Canada has reserved a parking spot for us so we can pull in and walk through a side door straight into our dressing room. That's going to make things a lot easier.

We might go out for dinner as a team a couple of times, and I will be making one appearance at the Brier Patch for an onstage interview, but that's about it for socializing.

And after the Brier?

I always come back to that line in Andre Agassi's autobiography, *Open*, where he writes, "Please let this be over. I'm not ready for it to be over." That is exactly how I feel. I can't wait for it to finish up, but I also know that I'm going to miss like crazy playing in the big events like the Brier and the trials.

During the tournament I know that I will be reflecting on the fact that it's my last Brier, and that's going to be incredibly sad. But I can't make the decision to continue for four more years based on one event because there are 355 days of the year where I've got to grind away and practise and train and travel and be away from my family and not do all of the other things that I want to do in my life.

I'm not going to lie. I'm a little worried about what life is going to be like after I leave competitive curling. I'm sure the first week or two is going to be refreshing and nice. But once the boredom of routine sets in, that's when it'll start hitting me that I've got to find something else to challenge myself.

In the short term, I'm going to be very busy following my girls as they compete.

The week after the Brier, I head to Corner Brook. Marissa is playing in the Canada Games qualifier there. The week after that, she will be off in P.E.I. playing in RockFest, which is a U-15 challenge for kids across the country.

And then the week after that, I'm off to Sudbury, where Hayley is playing in the national U-20s championships. (Looking way ahead, the Memorial University team that Hayley plays on won the Canadian U Sports championship, which means that we'll be following them to China for the Winter World University Games next January 2027.)

I'm looking forward to being an even more involved curling dad. But I know that at some point, things are going to slow down, and for the first time since I was a teenager, I won't be training or practising or chasing sponsors or planning travel or playing another season.

I think about that a lot. Outside of worrying about crying every day during the Brier, my biggest stress is wondering what comes next.

17

THE LAST DANCE

In the end, the 2026 Brier in St. John's was a very different experience for me than 2017. The emotions and the stress level were just as high, but for different reasons.

In 2017 we had never won a Brier. We were the number one team in the world, had been extremely dominant that whole season, were playing in front of our loyal, passionate fans in Newfoundland, and we felt the pressure to finally go out and win one.

But this time around, we came into the tournament after struggling through the season, and I think I was more nervous about the emotion surrounding my final Brier appearance than about how I was going to play.

Don't get me wrong—we all wanted to perform as well as we could, but I knew full well that we were not the best team in the world anymore. That said, if we played our absolute best, I felt there was a chance we could win. But for me the real pressure and the real nerves came from wondering how I was going to get through those ten days, knowing that it was probably my last competition.

The lead-up to the Brier was understandably busy because everyone wanted a little piece of us—the media, the sponsors, the fans.

There was never a chance to sit down and brace myself for what was coming emotionally.

Finally, a day or two before the Brier began, I didn't have anything on my schedule. That was the first time I slowed down and started to think about it, and that's when I started to get more emotional.

Everything was fine for our first practice session at the Mary Brown's Centre. I liked the ice and I was comfortable in the venue because I'd played there so many times before and had some great success there in the past.

But on the opening night, when I went out for our pre-game practice before our first game against Quebec, I remember thinking, *Oh my God, this is going to be really tough.* A half-hour before the game, the arena was already two-thirds full. And when we walked out on the ice, we got a huge ovation—for *practice.*

I remember going back to the dressing room and talking to Kate Boone, our massage therapist, and being a bit teary-eyed. "You'll get through this," she said. "You'll be fine."

When they introduced our team before the game, we got another long and loud ovation. The organizers held up the start of the games and the TSN broadcast for nine minutes waiting for things to calm down. The guys and I needed all nine minutes to compose ourselves.

When we finally started to play, it was pretty obvious that Jean-Michel Ménard's team wasn't at its best that night. We played pretty well, but they didn't really push us, and we came out with a comfortable win.

With that first game over, I realized that I could still play well even while I was feeling so many different emotions. I felt like I could take a breath.

There were some really nice moments during the week.

On the first Sunday, I was invited to the Brier Patch, where they played a tribute video featuring interviews with a lot of the players I had competed with and against over the course of my career—and then finishing with some words from Krista. A lot of people said some really kind things, and that meant a lot to me.

Then I sat down for an onstage conversation. The big room at the St. John's Convention Centre was jammed. Seeing the size of that crowd and how the fans responded to me was pretty awesome.

Monday night was also special. We got to play Nathan Young's up-and-coming Newfoundland rink. A Newfoundlander versus a Newfoundlander at a Brier played in Newfoundland and shown on national television. That's something that never could have happened earlier in my career.

Nathan and his team put a lot of pressure on us in the first half of that game, and that made for an entertaining match. Fortunately for us, I made a really good shot in the fifth end that turned the tide, and we got a little bit more comfortable in the second half to wrap up the win.

But the biggest highlight of that night for me actually came before that game even started. The day before the Brier, some of the Curling Canada people asked me if I would be okay if they honoured my daughter Hayley's Memorial University team, which had just won the Canadian U Sports championship—a first for a female team from Newfoundland. I was so happy that they wanted to do that.

What a great experience for those girls to be able to go out in front of a full house and hear the reception from the crowd. When they announced Hayley's name she got a really loud cheer, and I know she was thrilled with that.

Hayley's team—and Nathan Young's team—were both coached by Jeff Thomas, someone who has had a big impact on my career from the time I was nineteen years old right up to my retirement.

Jeff is a great curler—he represented Newfoundland in four Briers—and, as far as I'm concerned, is the best coach our province has ever produced. He started working with our team from a technical standpoint before we headed off to our first Canadian junior championships. There are not many people as good as he is at breaking down the curling delivery, and he knew mine and Mark's better than anybody.

Jeff couldn't travel with us in those days because he had a job and young kids at home and was still competing himself. But throughout the year he'd come down to the curling club and work with us.

After I missed the draw and we lost the Canadian juniors in Moncton, there were some people waiting to meet us at the St. John's airport when we arrived home. The first one to greet us when we got off the airplane was Jeff. There's a picture of Jeff hugging me that wound up on the front page of the St. John's *Telegram*. All the emotions of losing that game came back in that moment. I was fine on the flight home, but as soon as I started hugging Jeff, the tears flowed down my cheeks. And I remember Jeff saying to me, "I'll do whatever I can to get you back there and get you another chance."

He made that commitment to me and he followed through. The next season, Jeff worked with us so hard and took time out from his own life to travel with us so that we could be as good as we possibly could be. We improved so much from that 2020 juniors to the 2021 juniors, which of course we won.

After that there were a number of years when Jeff was our full-time coach. He was our fifth man at the 2021 Olympic trials and went to the 2022 Games with us as a coach.

Even when he wasn't formally coaching our team, I could call him and say, "Jeff, I'm struggling with my out-turn today. Can you come down and have a look and see what's going on?" That was the kind of relationship we've had.

Once Jeff retired and his kids moved away from home, he could spend more time at the curling club. Over five or six years he was at a lot of our practices, holding brooms and providing feedback to us on what we were doing. He was a big help.

I'm so glad that he's going to be coaching Hayley's team at the World University Games. He's the perfect guy for the job.

♣

When we played Nathan Young, I know there was some media conversation about how he was the "new Brad Gushue"—the next Newfoundland curler who was going to make his mark at the top of the sport. Even when we played the young Ontario rink, skipped by Jayden King, later in the week, there was a lot of talk about the next generation of great curlers coming along.

In fairness to Nathan, he is an extremely good player who had a very good accomplished junior career. If he decides to take the path that I've taken, I'm sure he will have a ton of success.

But I found it somewhat baffling when people compared him with me and our team. Because while Nathan has committed a lot to the game, I think it pales in comparison to what we had to do. And that's not a knock against Nathan. It's just that a lot of people underestimate what it takes to really compete and have no idea how much time and effort we put into the sport, especially in our late teens and throughout our twenties and early thirties—really, all the way up to today.

When you see some of these younger teams coming up and media commentators start talking about the next Kevin Koe or the next Gushue, I think they should be a bit more careful. It sets up expectations for those players that they don't need. They can be great teams if they want to be. But are they willing to do everything that our team did on and off the ice to be the best in the world?

Mark and I have talked about that narrative around the new generation of curlers. "If they only knew . . ." we always say to each other. If they did know, I don't think those comparisons would come out so quickly.

And times are different now.

At the beginning of our career, twenty, twenty-five years ago, travel was crazy expensive for us, but it's even more expensive now.

And the chance of breaking into the top of the world rankings today is even less than it was when we started out. At that time the talent was a little more diluted, because of team residency requirements, so it was a little easier to be competitive at a Grand Slam. As a twenty-year-old, you could go out and beat a top-ten team if you caught them on a bad day, because even the best teams always had one or two guys who were a little bit weaker than the rest. It was a realistic expectation.

Today, though, if you're a new team and you go up against a team that's ranked in the top ten in the world, it's difficult, if not impossible, to beat them because there has been such a concentration of all the top players. In Canada, we no longer have strict residency requirements for teams, which means the sport now has free agents and allows for the creation of "superteams," where the best curlers are consolidated into three, four, maybe five rinks at the most. When I first started to compete, that talent would be stretched over as many as fifteen teams.

And then there's the commitment and the sacrifice required. Curling was our whole life. We didn't take on the non-sports careers that we could have and didn't pursue the educational opportunities that might have been available to us. I probably would have gone to architecture school had I not been so committed to curling.

When you jump from junior to senior, it's a transformative time. If you take time off to pursue a career that doesn't allow you to take fifteen weeks off a year to curl, that developmental time is lost forever. And if you try to return to the sport later, you'll likely max out as a high-level club curler at best.

A young curler today who wants to follow the path that we did would either have to have their family support them financially, because they're not going to make a ton of money starting out, or they'll have to get really good really fast at selling themselves and their team to sponsors.

Consider those two young teams from Ontario and Newfoundland in the 2026 Brier. They made it that far but hadn't won anything at a senior level or even been on television. For them to attract a sponsor, they'd need to sell a dream of future success. That's not a *little* harder—it's *way* harder than selling results and selling championships and selling visibility.

I know that, because I was in that position when we were just starting out. Fortunately for me, I finally found a couple of people and companies who bought into my dream and bought into the vision I was selling. Those sponsors provided enough money to cover our expenses even if we didn't win immediately. That gave us a vital cushion so that we didn't have to risk losing all of our savings or asking our parents for loans.

When I first started looking for sponsors, I didn't love knocking on doors and I definitely didn't love the constant rejection. But I knew it was a necessary evil in order for us to succeed. I kept asking until I got a few yeses, and then once we had some success, it got a lot easier.

You also have to find teammates who not only are talented players but are just as committed as you are. That requires making some tough decisions. There are guys who say they are all-in, but when the time comes, are they going to be in the gym when they need to be in the gym? Are they going to be on the ice practising when you need them on the ice practising? Are they going to be able to put their own ego aside to make the team better? If you don't have all of those things in place, you've got to be willing to cut a guy. Feelings are going to get hurt and relationships are going to be severed.

The one thing I had throughout my whole career was a singular focus on being the best curler in the world.

It's going to be interesting and exciting to see which of these talented young players are going to have that same drive and be willing to do what it takes to get to the top and stay there.

We need some of those talented young players to stick with the game because some of our best players are approaching the end of their careers. If you looked at the 2026 Brier, the top four skips were all over forty—me, Mike McEwen, Brad Jacobs, and Kevin Koe. Right now, there isn't a twenty-five-year-old skip who can play at the level that we play at. And that's not bragging; that's just a fact. And one reason for that is that so many talented young curlers realize how hard it will be to get to our level and decide to pursue something else.

There is also a systemic issue with the funding in our sport that has prevented some players from committing to their careers. They know they're not going to make much money for the first five or six years, and that won't change (though, if it's successful, the new Rock League might help), but if there were an opportunity to grind through with a bit of financial help, I know there would be more curlers willing to sacrifice to get to the top.

Right now, a lot of our young athletes just don't see that happening. The funding from the Canadian government has hardly increased in the past twenty years, and the Own the Podium money, which we get through Curling Canada, has barely increased since the program came into being before the 2010 Olympics in Vancouver.

We get $1,800 a month from Sport Canada in "carding" money, which is non-taxable funding. (When I first got a card in 2006, it was

$1,500. That was only increased to $1,800 in 2017.) Expenses have obviously increased dramatically over the last twenty years, but the funding has stayed basically the same.

When you are in the early stages of your career and you realize that there's not loads of government support, you really have to focus on the corporate side. And corporate money is hard to come by when you have no experience. You're effectively asking companies to buy a lottery ticket, to take a huge chance that you'll turn out to be that one curling team that breaks through and gets a ton of exposure.

Meanwhile, the older guys, because they're still the best and they have their sponsors, are sticking around longer. Koe is going to keep playing, Jacobs is going to keep playing, McEwen is going to keep playing. By 2030, when the next Olympics roll around, McEwen will be fifty, Koe will be fifty-five, and Jacobs will be forty-five. And I don't blame them for hanging on. If they still love playing the game and they're still successful, why not keep going?

The only reason I decided to retire was because my passion for competing started to wane and I didn't get as much gratification from winning as I had in the past.

Ideally, we should have young guys pushing the old guys off the top of the podium. But that hasn't really happened, and some of the talented younger skips who have persevered just haven't been able to crack that elite level.

Brendan Bottcher was close at one point, and then he made the decision to form a team and that didn't really work out. Now that I have retired, he's coming back with his own rink as a skip, but he's certainly not viewed as having the same pedigree as me or Jacobs or Koe.

Tyler Tardi is moving back into the skipping role after playing four or five years with Koe, but he's really shown nothing at the men's level. And there's Rylan Kleiter, a young guy who had some success as a skip but who is now playing third for McEwen.

Within the curling world, this seems to be mostly a Canadian problem. Look at Scotland—Bruce Mouat is thirty-one, Ross Whyte is twenty-seven, and behind them you have James Craik who's only twenty-three. There are also some good young players coming up in other countries, like Marco Hoesli from Switzerland, who is twenty-six. They seem to bridge that gap between the juniors and seniors levels a whole lot better than we do in Canada.

But enough of that.

Back to the Brier.

♣

The one frustrating moment for our team during the round robin was our third game against Nova Scotia. Maybe a little bit of complacency was seeping in. Kendal Thompson's team had really struggled in their first couple of games, but we had played them a number of times in the past and we should have known they were good players. They were absolutely capable of beating us if we didn't play well. And we couldn't afford to let that game slip away if we wanted to finish first.

But for some reason we struggled. We weren't putting rocks in the right places. We weren't communicating on the ice. I felt like I was out there alone when the rock was coming down the sheet. I wasn't hearing anyone telling me what the weight was, which makes it really difficult to call the line. For some reason, our team just kind of went quiet.

It's not uncommon to have a game like that in the middle of a competition. When you play Briers and world championships and even the Olympics, sometimes you get halfway through the week and the energy drops. You lose the excitement that's been there for the first couple of games. The crowd is a little less intense than they were at the beginning. And you go through a bit of a lull before the excitement picks up again at the end of the week, when you can see the playoffs ahead of you.

At one point during the Nova Scotia game, the mic on the TSN broadcast picked up a between-ends conversation between me and our coach, Jeff Hoffart.

"We're not communicating out there," I complained.

The role of a coach is different on every team. We don't tend to use our coach to talk strategy. We use him to help manage our team. If I notice something happening that I don't like, having the coach there gives me someone to vent to other than my teammates. I can go over to him and say, "We're not talking the way we should. So-and-so is not doing this. We're not doing that."

The coach provides a buffer, a vehicle for me to get stuff off my chest without being confrontational. If necessary, he can pull a player aside and be more diplomatic than I would be. When you're in the middle of a game, and you get as intense as I do, sometimes you can be too direct.

I'm also sure there have been times when I've said things to coaches and they've brushed it off and never even bothered to approach the player I was complaining about because they knew I was just letting off steam. When you're out there on the ice for three hours, sometimes you just need someone to shoot the shit with, or to be able to complain to for the sake of complaining.

During the Brier, there is always one game that you probably shouldn't win that you do find a way to win—and you usually lose one that you shouldn't lose. That Nova Scotia game was one that I honestly don't think we deserved to win. It really came down to Kendal missing a simple hit in the ninth end. If he'd made that shot, we would have been down one with the hammer heading into the last end, with at best a fifty-fifty chance of winning the game. But he missed it, and all of a sudden we were up two and all but guaranteed the victory.

We walked away feeling like we had dodged a bullet, and it shifted our momentum. The team had a good conversation afterwards where we all acknowledged that we needed to communicate better. It was a one-game blip that we needed to address.

We managed much better after that. In our next game, against Nunavut, we actually wound up talking more than we needed to, but that's a better problem to have than being too quiet.

On the Wednesday night, I had another personal highlight. I had known for months that my daughter Marissa would be coming out with our team for the night's pre-game ceremonies as one of the "future stars"—junior curlers who walk out with the competing teams.

We generally give our "future stars" one of our jerseys to wear. All the other kids were super pumped to put theirs on, but I had to fight with Marissa to wear mine. She's a fourteen-year-old girl, and she was too cool for that. But she reluctantly gave in, and it was so much fun to have her out there and to hear the reception she got from the crowd.

Our team played really well that night to beat Saskatchewan 6–5 and move to 7–0 in the round robin with one game remaining.

That last one was against Brad Jacobs and Team Canada. Even before the Brier started, we knew that if both teams played the way they were capable of playing, that match was likely going to decide who would finish in first place in our pool.

We really wanted to put on a show for the people in St. John's and for the television audience. Jacobs was on a high, coming off winning the Olympics in Milan.

At the Grand Slam in St. John's the previous year, he had really embraced playing the heel in front of our home crowd. We knew it was going to be loud in the Mary Brown's Centre. But we weren't sure how the fans would react to Brad after the whole double-touching controversy and then winning gold for Canada.

To be honest, I thought they were very respectful and kind to him, even if the cheers we got were infinitely louder.

There was a different intensity to that game. I think it was the best I had played all week. I made some incredible shots that frustrated Brad's team—or at least that's what they told me afterwards.

The game came down to the tenth end. We were up two without the hammer, and for a while it looked like three might be in play for Jacobs. I made a good hit and roll with my first shot, which eliminated that chance, and then I made a double on my last to get rid of both of their rocks and win the game.

When I made that shot, the roar in the building was almost as intense as it was when I made my Brier-winning shot in 2017. But this time, all that was at stake was finishing first in the round robin and having the hammer entering the playoffs—which gave us a pretty good leg up.

Our first playoff game was against Matt Dunstone. We were in control for most of it, but we just couldn't stretch our lead. We were one up, tied, one up, tied—we could never get that two- or three-point lead. Matt's team was making some good shots and hanging with us.

We got to the last end up one without the hammer. Their team positioned some rocks really well, leaving us with a bunch of bad angles. We missed one of Brendan's shots, and then one of Mark's got us in a little bit of trouble. Matt was going to have a shot to score two and win the game, whether it was an out-turn angle raise or a short in-turn angle raise.

On my last rock, I was trying to guard a very short in-turn angle raise and I wanted to make sure I didn't get my guard too tight because that would have allowed Matt to run that rock back in. To be honest, I overthought the shot, because if I had just gone ahead and thrown that rock six or eight feet harder, the odds of Matt making his shot weren't great.

Instead, I underthrew it. The guys swept it the whole way but it stopped, biting the hog line, and was pulled off. That left Matt a shot that he's going to make almost every time.

It was my mistake. I gave Matt too much respect. If I had just thrown a halfway guard, we probably would have wound up going to an extra end.

Needless to say, I was pretty frustrated by the result. I felt I'd thrown a good rock. I was a little surprised that it didn't make it over the hog line because I didn't feel that I threw it that lightly. Maybe it just took a bit of a different path and came up light.

I kept second-guessing myself. Why did I think I had to be that high or that close to the hog line?

But I had to put that behind me and move on.

Because of the way the playoff format worked, the worst part of losing the game to Matt Dunstone was that it meant we would now have to win four games in a row against really good teams to win the Brier. Even though we had finished the round robin undefeated and had only that one playoff loss against a top-five team, our chances were now hanging by a thread.

Our second playoff game was against Ontario's talented Jayden King.

I could tell that Jayden and his team were pretty nervous. I'm sure they were happy just to have made it to the playoffs, but I could tell they weren't really comfortable. That's part of the reason I felt so confident going into that game. The Ontario team played well, but I knew that as the game went on, we were going to separate ourselves from them, and that's what happened.

That was Friday night.

Saturday afternoon, we were right back on the ice facing Brad Jacobs again. And now we were the only game in the building, playing in front of a full house against a team that had been our nemesis for a long time.

I didn't like what I saw from our team throughout that game. It felt like we were nervous out there, to be quite honest. And I think it was the first time that it really started to sink in that this game could be my last. I had a hard time battling that feeling and fighting it off.

Brad's team came out playing well, and I had to make two tough shots in the first end just to score a single. In the second, I had to make two more shots so that we didn't give up two or three.

Through the first five ends, I played incredibly well and made some great shots just to keep us close. Heading into the sixth end, we were tied at two but they had the hammer.

I was waiting and waiting for our guys to come around. Instead, we played another sloppy end, and I was going to have to make a really difficult freeze on my last shot to keep them from scoring two or three. But we miscalled the line and I feather-ticked the guard, leaving Brad a simple double for three.

Needless to say, he made it.

That's when the emotion really kicked in. I realized that with being down three points with only four ends left against a team as good as Brad's, the odds of us winning were slim. These were almost certainly going to be the last four ends of my career.

I fought hard to control how I was feeling. I wanted to take some moments to look around at the crowd and savour the experience, but I also wanted to give those last four ends everything I had. If there was a 10 percent chance of winning, I wanted to make sure that we found that 10 percent.

Our team started to play better and make a few more shots. After getting a deuce, we came into the last end down one without the hammer.

When I threw my first rock, we were still in a good situation. But I was a little bit heavy with my throw and left Jacobs a triple, which he made.

That left me with a hit and roll, which, even if I threw it perfectly, would leave Brad with a simple four- or five-foot runback.

My hit and roll was perfect. Brad couldn't see any of it. I remember going down to Geoff and Mark and saying, "If that's my last shot, at least it's a pretty good one."

When Jacobs threw his last rock, I could sense a little bit of anxiety in his and Marc Kennedy's voices, and I thought for just a second, *Maybe he missed it.*

But then the rock hit, and I knew it was done.

That's when it really hit me. I shifted out of competition mode and into thinking about how I was going to handle the next five, ten, twenty minutes.

Brad came up to me, shook my hand, and said something that was unexpected and really kind: "You're the best, ever."

Ben and Marc and Brett also had some really kind things to say, and I wished them good luck for the rest of the week.

I embraced the guys on our team and thanked them. And then I knew I had to face everybody and everything else—face the TV interview, face my family. I knew it was going to be intense.

When we got down to the other end of the sheet I hugged Mark, Brendan, and Geoff and said to them, "You guys go ahead." I hung back with Adam Casey, who was our fifth man, and then walked down the ice with him because I didn't want to walk alone.

Bryan Mudryk from TSN was waiting for me, but before the interview they asked the crowd to watch the big screen in the arena. I had no idea what the video was going to be like. But I knew that I couldn't focus on it because if I did, I probably wouldn't be able to get through the interview without breaking down.

(I did get to watch the video afterwards. Kevin Pratt and TSN did an amazing job putting it together. It was a special piece.)

When the video ended Bryan came up to me, and all I can remember thinking was, *Don't cry, don't cry, don't cry*.

I got through it pretty well. I know I didn't get to say everything I wanted to say and thank everyone I wanted to thank, but I showed my appreciation to my family and my teammates and our support staff who had been with me through all of it.

And then things got really awkward. The crowd was standing and cheering and they just kept on standing and cheering, and I didn't know when to leave.

The truth is, I didn't want to leave—because once I left, that would be it. It would be over.

I held it together until I saw Krista and my parents. I don't think I've ever seen my dad as emotional as he was that night. That hit me really hard.

I'm not sure how long I stood there. Maybe two minutes. Maybe twenty. I really don't know.

Finally, it felt like the right time to walk off the ice.

Looking back over that Brier, I think I actually did pretty well.

I got through the first game and realized that I could handle all the emotions and still play well. I was named the second all-star skip, and with the exception of Kevin Koe playing the best I've ever seen him play, I probably was the top skip there—and skips win championships.

Right up until that sixth end against Jacobs when I missed my last rock and touched the guard, we had a very realistic chance to win.

If I had made that shot, we probably would have had the steal, and we would have been one up after six instead of being down by three.

But we didn't make it. That's the fine line you ride. The best teams are so good that sometimes it all comes down to mis-sweeping one rock. Even in the game against Dunstone, it came down to that little underthrow. If only I'd thrown four feet more than I did . . .

We ended up finishing fourth. Do I think we were the fourth-best team out there? Absolutely not. We were definitely better than that. It all came down to those two shots that I'd love to have back.

But saying that we could have won is different than saying we *should* have won.

Starting in about 2011, I felt I was the best player in the world. I felt that way until the last year.

Since 2015, I believed we were the best team in the world. And I think that was true until the beginning of the 2024–25 season.

When we were firing on all cylinders from 2016 through 2024, we didn't need a whole lot of breaks. We'd just go out and play well and we'd win. I knew that if I played my best, I was going to outplay anyone in the world.

The last year and a half, it has been a different story.

Over those final two seasons it felt as if we needed someone to miss a shot—or maybe we had to get a little bit lucky.

It's natural to lose a step or two when you get older. The skills fade away and some of the motivation dwindles and that adds up to the difference between believing that you're going to win every game and losing the close ones.

And that's what happened to me in St. John's.

The hours immediately after that last game weren't so bad. My immediate family came down to the dressing room, and then we all headed out to Quidi Vidi Breweries, where they had set up a space for all of our family and friends. We had a chill night, ordered some food, had a couple of beers, and when I finally got home, I was exhausted, like being tired after a long day's work.

When I woke up the next morning, the girls wanted to go down to watch the final and I decided to go with them. That's when the end of my career started to feel a bit more real.

When I got to the rink, I had the opportunity to acknowledge some people who I didn't get a chance to thank the night before. There are a bunch of guys who were on the camera crew that would travel with the Sportsnet and TSN broadcasts. They'd been covering my career ever since it started and I wanted to thank them for being good buddies who I could talk to over the years.

I also wanted to thank everybody around the Brier—the volunteers, the Curling Canada crew, and certainly the chairpersons for putting on such an amazing event. It was run incredibly well with huge energy throughout the week.

After getting through all of the thank-yous, I sat down and watched the final—which hit me pretty hard. When it got to the end and Matt made his shot to win, I admit that I felt a bit of envy.

I wanted to be that guy one more time.

I think what I'm going to remember most about my curling life, outside of hanging out with my teammates, is playing in the Brier. There's nothing else quite like it.

If I could play the Brier every week, I probably wouldn't retire. I love it so much. I love the atmosphere, love the event, and love the crowds.

Seeing how everyone embraced Matt and his team after they won, I couldn't help but think: *I'm really going to miss this.*

18

APRIL 5, 2026

After the Brier, I really didn't have a chance to sit down and take it all in. Two days later, I was off to Corner Brook to watch Marissa play for the right to represent Newfoundland in the 2027 Canada Games qualifier (her team won). I came home for a day or two and then travelled to P.E.I., again with Marissa, for the U-15 RockFest (she finished second).

Today I'm headed for Sudbury to see Hayley play again, this time with the Newfoundland team in the Canadian U-20 championship. I haven't been away from curling long enough to really process the idea that my playing career is at an end.

Since the Brier, I've been following what has been happening with other teams, the comings and goings that always take place at the end of the Olympic quadrennial. I had an inside track with the guys on our team, so I knew what was coming, but there have been some moves on other teams that really surprised me.

Spring is always a fun time in the sport. There is a lot of hope, a lot of enthusiasm for the season to come. You form a new team and you get excited thinking this could be the year that gets you over the line.

But now I'm on the outside looking in, and it feels different.

On one hand, I'm kind of relieved. It can become all-consuming for players. Your head is racing around. You're having different conversations. You're trying to take in all the information and create a team that you feel gives you the best chance to go to the Olympics. Sometimes you talk to players, seven, eight, ten times. A lot goes into forming a team.

Everybody is gung-ho to get their new team started, and I do miss that feeling of joy and that anticipation that comes with creating a new team.

I was happy I wasn't part of it, but I was also sad that I wasn't part of it.

I did get to dip my toes in as Brendan and Geoff kept me up to date on what they were hearing and what people were saying. I look at some of the moves that teams and players have made and wonder what they were thinking. Are they really committing for all four years? Will they be playing fewer events or more events? Some of those teams probably figure that they'll just try to get to the Brier and see what happens. But I know that others are going to go all in and devote themselves 110 percent. It really depends on what their goals are.

When you hear players talking about their new team and what their plans are, you can usually tell what they're thinking.

If they don't want to compete in many events, you know they're playing just because they love the game and want to be around it. Maybe they have other interests in their lives. They might have kids that are at a certain age and they don't want to be away as much. Maybe they have a job that doesn't allow them to travel as much.

They might be four great players and the team might look good on paper, but I can tell when they're not really committed.

And then you see other teams get together where there are four guys all at a similar stage in their lives, usually on the younger side, who can really sink their teeth in and go hard. They're going to play a lot because they have to generate enough points to get into the Grand Slams and some of the bigger events. That also tells me that they've got their sights set on the Olympics or winning the Brier.

We didn't play a lot the last few years because we had developed such good routines that we knew we could play less and still be competitive. It takes years before you become comfortable enough as a team and comfortable enough in different situations that you don't need to be out there every week.

But for the younger, ambitious teams, they have to go out and play if they're serious about it. They have to take their lumps and they have to learn.

When I formed the team with Geoff, Brett, and Mark we had two, three, four years where we played as much as or more than anybody. We were playing two out of every three weeks. Obviously, we made sure we played all the big events—the Canada Cups, the Continental Cups, the Slams—but in between those we would fit in whatever worked best. We ended up in some pretty small places in Canada playing events that didn't have the biggest purses, but that was what we felt we needed to do to expedite our learning curve as a team.

There are so many nuances in the game of curling. There's so much learning you have to do to get to the point where everything clicks. You have to experience those pressure moments where you're playing in a final or semifinal and learn from them. That's the only way to prepare for the time when the TV lights are on and you're playing in the last end of a Brier final.

I do love the move that Brendan and Geoff made, teaming up with the Horgan brothers, Jacob and Tanner. They've added two great young players who are only going to get better over the next four years. Often, in any sport, big free-agent signings are based on a player's history—what they've done—rather than their future and what they might be able to do. With the Horgans, I think their best years are ahead of them, so I'm excited for Brendan and Geoff to have them on board.

As far as the other teams go, Mike McEwen got cut by his guys, but I think he's landed in a really good spot hooking up with Saskatchewan's Ryan Kleiter and some young players who are incredibly good sweepers. He had one great sweeper before on his team in Colton Flasch and now he's got two, with Trevor Johnson and Joshua Mattern, which means you're going to see some really good curling from Mike. He'll have a much bigger window to throw in.

Matt Dunstone just made it to the final at the world championships where he lost to Niklas Edin. There was a lot of speculation of what he was going to do with E.J. retiring—a lot of it focused on Mark Nichols. Mark didn't tell us anything about his plans. I thought he might decide to retire. I didn't know that he was joining Matt's team until I saw it on social media along with everyone else. I admit that Geoff and I were a bit surprised that he didn't give us a heads-up.

Any time you can join the reigning Canadian champions, it has to be a pretty good move. They have lots of talent, and the other guys are young and hungry. Joining Dunstone gives Mark a good chance to continue winning, and another season might help him to determine if he wants to continue playing or step away from the game. I can't imagine that he made a four-year commitment to them, but with Mark's resumé, Team Dunstone would have been silly not to take him, even if he just wanted to go year to year.

And then there's Brad Jacobs. Marc Kennedy and Ben Hebert have decided to play for one more year, through next year's Brier in Regina. If they retire after that, we could see a huge shakeup that would send ripples through as many as three or four teams.

But by the time that plays out, I will already have been a year into my retirement.

Usually at the end of the season, I hit the gym right away, without any real break. I'd get home from the Brier on a Monday and I'd be back working out by Wednesday or Thursday.

I would normally take time away from the ice, but by August I'd be excited to get back to the rink.

This year, I watched the Brier final Sunday night, and on Monday morning I was back in the gym with my trainer, as usual. I think it was just as much for my mental health as my physical health. The workouts might not be as intense as they've been in the past, but it's important for me to continue with them.

The uncertainty about what I'm going to do next has been difficult for me.

I've enrolled in a program called Success Beyond Sports that the Canadian Olympic Committee offers through its Game Plan program. It focuses on how former athletes can reinvent themselves. Some of the routines that helped make you a great athlete aren't necessarily going to work the same way in the next stage of your life. You have to step back and analyze yourself. What do I do really well? What are some of the strengths and values that I have that are going to translate into a different kind of life, and which ones aren't?

I was the best curler in the world for a long time. No matter what I do from now on, I'm going to be starting at the bottom. I'm not going to jump in and be the best in the world, whether it's in a business or coaching or broadcasting or something else. I'm going to have to learn what I need to do to be successful, and I understand that's going to be a difficult process.

I need to find something that I love to do and that's going to keep me motivated to get up every morning trying to be better. Right now, I have no idea what that is. I'm searching, but I'm also trying to give myself time. I don't need to find the next adventure right away, but over the next six months I'd love to choose a direction.

Whatever it is, I know it's unlikely that I'll have the same passion for it that I've had for curling over the past thirty years.

I'm forty-five years old. When I was twenty, curling was everything to me. I don't think I'm ever going to have that kind of singular focus again—in part because if I did, it would take away from the things I want to do with my family. They are priority number one. Whatever comes next doesn't need to be so all-encompassing. I've been there and done that with the obsessive part, the positives and the negatives.

I'm hoping my life can be a little more balanced now. I want to be able to travel with the girls wherever they're competing. I was talking to Krista about the opportunities that I've missed over the last twenty-five years. Some of it is little stuff, like a vacation somewhere warm in the winter, which every Canadian loves because it's so cold here, especially in Newfoundland. I've never been able to do that during the curling season. The same with skiing. I haven't skied since I was a teenager because the season coincided with curling and because there was always a high risk of injury. I'd love to do all of those things that I've missed out on because I've never been able to take the time for them. They may seem very small, the kind of stuff other people take for granted, but I'm genuinely excited about those possibilities.

That's for later.

Right now, I don't think I'm done with the grieving process quite yet. I realize now what it feels to grieve for your past life, remembering everything the guys and I went through to be on top of the world and the incredible feeling of being celebrated by the fans.

I'm not going to lie—all that was really cool. But now I've got to come to terms with finding a new role or a new job where there aren't going to be six thousand people standing up and cheering for me when I make a shot to win a game.

When next season starts, am I going to miss that as much as I think I will?

I know I'm going to miss the Brier. I'm going to miss hanging out with the guys. I'm going to miss that competitive edge.

Those are the experiences and the feelings that I'm going to have to try to replace in some way, shape, or form. I am concerned about how to fill the void that's going to be left. A lot of the thoughts in my head have revolved around curling. What are they going to be about now? What am I going to shift all my attention to? If I don't find something, I think I'm going to drive myself crazy.

I know it's not going to be easy.

19

AN EXTRA END

The main reason I announced my retirement early was to give the guys on our team a big window to make sure that they found a good spot to play next season. I was also hoping that it would create an opportunity for people who might see me as a good fit for a job that could become part of my post-playing career.

But as the year went on, I was a bit surprised that I hadn't heard much of anything about other opportunities.

And then a day or two before the Brier, I got a text from Dean Gemmell, who's the CEO of U.S. Curling, letting me know that they were posting a job for a new high-performance director. "I'd love to see you apply," Dean said.

I wrote back and told him that I wasn't going to even think about the job until after the Brier was finished. Dean got in touch again a couple of weeks after the tournament, and I admit that my initial reaction was that I wasn't interested.

But then I decided that it would be a good exercise to at least go through the interview process. I talked to Dean a bit more about the job, and I also talked to Gerry Peckham, who was the high-performance director at Curling Canada for thirty-three years. Gerry said that he thought the role was a perfect fit for me because I have the curling expertise and I also have my MBA, which would be an asset with the business and administrative side of the job.

But I did wonder what the reaction would be because of the tension with the United States right now. As Canadians, we are rightly and understandably angry about threats to our sovereignty. Would that trickle down to my personal situation? Would there be a backlash at home? How big could it be?

I always came back to the fact that taking this job wasn't a political statement. It was simply about finding a post-playing career while doing what was best for me and Krista and the girls.

All of us in Canada know someone who has had to move to the States to pursue a work opportunity—including in sports—and there has always been a lot of movement back and forth between the two countries. There are Canadian hockey players down in the U.S., and there are Canadian coaches working with U.S. teams in a variety of different sports, and vice versa. Canadians have always had a close affiliation with the Americans, and I believe that is probably going to continue once we get through this difficult period.

This position will allow me to do something I think I am going to love—to stay involved in curling while maintaining a degree of flexibility that is important at this stage in my life and career.

Most importantly, I'll be able to do most of my work from home in Newfoundland and to be around my kids and my wife after all of those years spending so much time on the road.

Should I turn down a great job opportunity just because there will be some people who might not like it? I've already made a lot of those types of compromises. For most of my career—especially the second half of it—I had to make decisions that were based on how the public would react because we were trying to attract and keep sponsors.

I understand that some people might be disappointed, but I hope that when they look at it from my perspective, they'll understand. That's all I can ask. I can't control how they feel.

I'm not worried about blowback within curling circles. There's going to be zero pushback from players because they understand how small the curling world is and how few jobs there actually are.

I love curling. I still want to be around the sport, and this is a role that will give me the ability to change the career paths for both players and coaches. This job wasn't available to me in Canada. (David Murdoch—a Scot, by the way—succeeded Gerry Peckham in 2023 and has done great work.) Given that Curling Canada has only had two high-performance directors in thirty-seven years, it's safe to say that those opportunities at home don't come along every day.

That's why I accepted the job with U.S. Curling.

As they say, when it rains, it pours.

Not long afterwards, I got a call from The Curling Group asking me if I would be interested in working with Rogers Sportsnet on the broadcasts of the Grand Slam events.

That felt like a great opportunity. The Grand Slams have been a huge part of my career over the last twenty years. And they have always been fun events.

The job will allow me to try my hand at broadcasting, which has always been something I've been interested in pursuing once my playing career was finished. And the two roles fit together—The Curling Group was fine with me taking on the role with U.S. Curling, and by being at the Grand Slams I'd have a chance to watch the top players in the world, stay on top of what is happening, and see how the U.S. teams are performing. There are a lot of synergies.

I'm a little nervous about the on-air part of the job. I've only done commentary twice before, and I was kind of thrown into the fire with no real preparation. I hope the folks at Rogers Sportsnet give me at least a few dress rehearsals before I go on air for the first time. But I know the game so well, and I'm so comfortable talking about what's happening on the ice, that I think some of the information I can provide viewers is going to be insightful. It's just a matter of getting comfortable and knowing when to jump in and when to stay quiet. I'm sure they will have some good teachers who can help me with that.

As I was going through the process with U.S. Curling and then The Curling Group, I also received a message from Devin Heroux at the CBC, wondering what my plans were.

I first got to know Devin during the 2017 Brier, where he did a really great job covering the event, especially on Twitter. I had a lot of friends who couldn't make it down to the venue and followed Devin religiously to see what was happening on the ice. He's the kind of reporter who isn't afraid to ask some different questions. He gets very much into the emotional side of the game, what you're feeling as an athlete. I have always found his perspective very interesting.

We struck up a mutually respectful relationship over the years. He was a journalist and I was an athlete, but we had some good conversations that extended far beyond our respective roles.

Devin had been doing a podcast with Colleen Jones called *That Curling Show*. For someone of my generation, Colleen was an idol. She was from Nova Scotia, a fellow Atlantic Canadian, whose teams had a ton of success, including winning six Scotties. Over the years I got to know her really well. I loved Colleen and had a tremendous amount of respect for her.

Sadly, Colleen passed in November 2025. Devin asked me if I had any interest in being a contributor to the podcast. I was honoured and flattered that he thought of me. I knew Colleen would want the show to go on. The podcast will be a different kind of media job than what I was taking on with The Curling Group—not analyzing a game, but talking about the sport from a completely different angle. And I would be working with a good colleague who I know will help me hone my skills.

So that was an easy yes for me.

Now it's time to try these new things. Some of them I'm going to love, and no doubt some of them I'm not going to love quite as much.

Up until now, my working life has been all curling, all the time. The sport has been my north star since I was a teenager. Everything that I did and every decision I made revolved around how it was going to affect my game and help me become the best curler in the world. Now that I have stepped away from competing, I don't have that north star anymore, and I'm not really sure what goal I'm working towards. But eventually I know I'm going to find it.

It may be as simple as being around my family and having the flexibility to follow my girls' careers, to be the girls' dad when they need me. But I think it's also going to be important to have my own personal aspirations and career goals. I just have to figure out what those are.

I still have at least twenty working years ahead of me and I want to do something I'm passionate about. In a lot of ways, it's similar to what my daughter Hayley is going through right now. She's in university and eventually she's going to have to choose a program that will have a huge impact on her future career. There's so much uncertainty at her stage in life. You want to find something that is going to keep you happy and motivated and let you become the best version of yourself, but at the same time you don't really know what you like or don't like yet because you haven't been able to experience different things.

Hayley's twenty and I'm forty-five, and here we are in the exact same place.

ACKNOWLEDGMENTS

Writing this book has been a fun and rewarding process, and I am grateful to the many people who helped make it possible.

First, thank you to Stephen Brunt, my co-author, who made the process not only manageable but genuinely enjoyable. Stephen asked all the right questions, organized my thoughts, shaped the stories, and made what could have been a difficult process feel very comfortable. From our first dinner together in Woody Point, we had an immediate connection. I am grateful not only for his talent and professionalism but for his friendship.

I am also grateful to Scott Sellers, my publisher and editor, who believed in this book from the beginning. His steady guidance with every draft helped bring it to life. Throughout the writing, Scott eased my mind and helped build my confidence in the work we were doing. His support has meant a great deal to me.

I would also like to thank Kristin Cochrane, Marion Garner, and Adria Iwasutiak at Penguin Random House Canada for all their support.

To my wife, Krista, thank you for being with me through the good and the bad. You have been my best friend, my biggest fan, and the person who has taken on so much so that I could follow my dream.

I love you more than I can ever properly express, and I would not have wanted to go through this journey with anyone else. Through the pressures, the sacrifices, the disappointments, and the greatest moments of my career, you were the first person I wanted to talk to and the person I wanted beside me.

To my children, Hayley and Marissa, thank you for giving me perspective, joy, and purpose. Winning on the ice has brought me a lot of pride, but nothing has made me prouder than being your dad. I hope I have made you proud as well.

To my mom and dad, Ray and Maureen, thank you for introducing me to sport and for doing everything you could to allow me to pursue my dream of becoming the best in the world. More than that, thank you for teaching me the importance of hard work, and giving me the values that have guided me throughout my life and career. The example you both set shaped not only the competitor I became, but the person I try to be every day. I love you both, and I appreciate all the sacrifices you made over the years, and the belief you had in me from the very beginning.

To my sister, Natasha, thank you for being there at the very beginning of my curling journey. In many ways, you were the person I started this whole thing with, and I probably would not have started curling without you. I will always be grateful that we shared those first steps together.

I also want to thank Krista's parents, Harvey and Marie, for everything they have done for our family over the years. So often, when I was on the road competing or training, they stepped in to help care for the girls and look after the house. Their support gave Krista and me peace of mind during some of the busiest and most demanding times of my career, and I am deeply grateful for everything that you've done.

To all my teammates over the years, there are too many of you to list, but each of you played an important part in all of the success we shared on the ice. You pushed me to be better, challenged me when I needed it, and helped create an environment where I could make mistakes, learn, and grow as a leader. The wins, the championships, and the memories were never mine alone.

To Mark, thank you for being there longer than anyone. We've shared so much—so many pressure moments, long seasons, tough losses, and unforgettable wins. Your loyalty, commitment, and belief in what we were building meant more than I probably said along the way.

To Geoff, thank you for bringing so many qualities to our team that I did not always have myself. Your patience, calmness, steadiness, and ability to keep perspective made us better. You balanced me, grounded our team during important moments, and played a huge role in our success together.

Thank you to Jeff Thomas, my longtime coach, who watched me grow up and helped me become the player I am. To Toby McDonald, thank you for your guidance and the role you played in my growth as both a curler and a person. To Kate Boone, our massage therapist, thank you for becoming a close friend and for all the times you helped me to get back on the ice. You are a great listener, someone I could talk through the pressures and frustrations with during the long stretches on the road.

I am also grateful to the sponsors who supported my teams and me along the way, including Maple Leaf Foods, GIP Atlantic, Kubota, Eastlink, Oxford Frozen Foods, Connect Hearing, Dennis Langdon of RMS, Arnold Asham of Asham Curling Supplies, and Erin Flowers of Goldline Curling Supplies. Your belief and support have meant so much over the years.

Finally, thank you to everyone who has been part of this journey—family, friends, coaches, teammates, sponsors, fans, and supporters. This career, and this book, would not have been possible without you.